We have lived and have lived to bee good to oureselves and others, our sowles which are putt into the sturring earthe of our bodyes have atcheved the causes of theyre hether coming, they have knowne and honoured with knowledg the cause of theyre Creation: And for many men (for in this tyme place and fortune yt ys lawfull for us to speake gloriusly) yt hathe been behovefull that we shoulde live.

Sir Philip Sidney

to Ethel Seaton
in gratitude

NOTE ON TEXTS

I have used the following editions for references to the more important writers:

CHAUCER: *Works*, ed. A. W. Pollard, 1919.
MALORY: *Works*, ed. E. Vinaver, 3 vols., 1947.
SIDNEY: *Complete Works*, ed. A. Feuillerat, 4 vols., 1923.
SPENSER: *Poetical Works*, ed. J. C. Smith and E. de Selincourt, 1912.
MILTON: *Poetical Works*, ed. H. C. Beeching, 1932.

References to the publications of the Early English Texts Society are abbreviated to E.E.T.S.

CONTENTS

INTRODUCTION: THE CLUE OF LANGUAGE   13

I   BRAVE AND GLORIOUS WORDS   *page* 15

II   VERTUOUS NOBLESSE   28

III   THE DREAM OF SIR THOMAS MALORY   46

IV   THAT MOST HEROICKE SPIRIT   62

V   TH'ETERNALL BROOD OF GLORIE   75

VI   MAGNANIMOUS TO CORRESPOND WITH HEAVEN   94

VII   LIGHT OF COMMON DAY   112

Introduction

THE CLUE OF LANGUAGE

The purpose of this book is very simple. It attempts no more than to pick up a verbal clue in the work of certain English writers, which may help to lead us back into the medieval and renaissance world through the study of a particular concept.

In any given period we may find certain words, representing general ideas, which are used casually again and again, as if everyone were aware of their meaning. Yet if we attend carefully to the context in which they occur, we shall find that the actual significance has subtly changed, diminished, or enlarged. We are familiar, for instance, with the mutations of the word 'democratic' in the last half-century. We know that when we speak of 'democratic behaviour' we do not mean quite the same thing as when we speak of 'democratic government'. We take our contemporary usages for granted, especially when they relate to a concept fundamental to our way of life. Words of this kind, or groups of words closely related to the same concept, may occur so frequently in certain periods that we feel them to be of particular significance as a clue to the intellectual, spiritual, and emotional world of the time.

Such a word is 'magnanimity' in the Middle Ages and the Renaissance. It is in frequent use from the twelfth to the early seventeenth centuries, with varying emphasis and shades of meaning, but always with reference to some generally accepted standard of conduct. But from the seventeenth century onwards it is used less and less, and comes less and less to refer to any general social concept. Gradually it diminishes to the name of just one among many other private virtues, such as honesty or sobriety.

Have we, in this, lost more than a mere word? Is there also some quality so far faded from our world and our literature that we find it hard to recognize in the writings of men long dead, so that when they would speak to us over the abysm of time we cannot clearly hear what they are saying? There are words of this kind which, studied with a deliberate and disciplined effort of the mind and imagination, will blow off the dust of past centuries and reveal more than would the most careful sociological study. If we can come to at least some understanding of the importance of 'magnanimity' to the world of the Middle Ages and the Renaissance, we shall have come one step nearer to valid communication with their writers.

This book makes no claim to originality, except in so far as every reader's response to an author is in some way peculiarly his own. But it is hoped that it may be of some use to the general reader who has little access to more scholarly works, which are generally confined to great libraries, or the young student whose reading in the period has not yet been very extensive. For this reason I have quoted freely from writers whose books are not readily available. I have normalized the typography of some of the early texts, while retaining the original spelling. The latter presents little difficulty to an intelligent reader, and without it some of the flavour of the original is lost. I have, however, provided glosses and translations where these seemed likely to be useful.

Chapter One

BRAVE AND GLORIOUS WORDS

The 'trivium' (grammar, logic, and rhetoric) of the seven liberal arts studied at a medieval university is a commonplace to students of education; and logic to the medieval student was almost synonymous with Aristotle. The study of 'this noble Philosopher Aristotelle', as Sir Thomas Elyot calls him, dominates formal European scholarship until the sixteenth century. In a letter to his younger brother Robert, in which he is chiefly concerned with a young man's duty to prepare himself for the service of his country, Sir Philip Sidney writes:

> I thinke you have read Aristotles Ethicks if you have, you knowe it is the begyning, and foundacion of all his Workes, the good end (to) which everie man doth and ought to bend his greatest actions (III, p. 124).

The context of this remark is significant, for Aristotle's purpose in his *Ethics* was to discover the principles of human conduct as a basis for political theory. It is natural for man to pursue happiness, and he finds happiness to be synonymous with the good life. The function of the state is to create conditions in which it is possible for the citizens to pursue such goodness, so it is important that we should understand what man's real nature is. In his treatise, therefore, Aristotle investigates the moral and political nature of man, whose virtues are the 'mean' between the two extremes of excess and deficiency:

15

It is in the nature of moral qualities that they can be destroyed by deficiency on the one hand and excess on the other. . . . The man who shuns and fears everything and can stand up to nothing becomes a coward. The man who is afraid of nothing at all, but marches up to every danger, becomes foolhardy. In the same way the man who indulges in every pleasure without refraining from a single one becomes incontinent. If, on the other hand, a man behaves like the Boor in comedy and turns his back on every pleasure, he will find his susceptibilities becoming blunted. So also temperance and courage are destroyed both by excess and deficiency, and they are kept alive by the observance of the mean[1] (II, ii).

In a series of 'case studies' in which the constituents of character are analysed – the Courageous Man, the Liberal Man, and so forth – Aristotle attempts to find the ideal of human behaviour. Probably he did no more than voice the opinion of any educated Greek of the fourth century B.C. His originality was that he made tacit assumptions into an explicitly formulated system and, without having the terms of modern psychology at his disposal, was yet able to turn the study of human conduct into a science. Many of his ideas became the commonplaces of Western thought, and one of the most influential was his picture of the Magnanimous Man.

Aristotle's own word for the virtue which he here describes is *megalopsychia* – high-mindedness. Modern translators tend to use 'proper pride', thereby stressing the great man's rightful consciousness of merit. Certainly, being truly great, he recognizes his own desert, stands on his dignity among his peers (though courteous and unassuming

[1] *Ethics*, trans. J. A. K. Thomson, Penguin Classics, 1953. (This edition is particularly helpful to the student with little previous knowledge of Aristotle.)

in his bearing towards humble people), is more willing to bestow benefits than to receive them, and cannot tolerate an undeservedly inferior position. He is one whom his inner resources make independent, so that he is equally indifferent to good and evil fortune. Yet in the completed picture the stress should be less on pride than on desert:

> The truly superior man must be a good man. Indeed, greatness in all the virtues is surely what stamps him for what he is. . . . Greatness of soul is the beautiful completion of the virtues, for it adds to them its own greatness and is inseparable from them (IV, vii).

Evidently *megalopsychia* is a transcendent quality, a wholeness of virtue, of which proper pride is but an accidental consequence.

The Latin equivalent of *megalopsychia* is *magnanimitas*. Here begins one of those subtle modifications of meaning to which words are subject. For the 'animus', which is one of its elements, can refer either to 'soul' or 'courage'. Hence the idea of greatness of spirit is fused with or sometimes substituted for that of courage – a great heart rather than greatness of thought. Cicero uses the word in this sense in his *De Officiis* (I, 19); but he is careful to distinguish it from self-seeking, personal ambition, or foolhardy rashness. At the end of the eleventh century, Hildebert of Lavardin, following Cicero, insists that *magnanimitas* is a quality of devotion to the public good rather than of personal glory. He refers to it as *virtus* or 'courage'.

> Haec virtus, cum ad aspera ineunda aliquem promptum faciat, communem utilitatem quam suam potius attendit. Sicut enim scientia, quae est remota a justitia, potius quam sapientia est appellanda calliditas; sic animus ad pericula paratus, si sua

cupiditate non communi utilitate impellitur, temeritatis potius nomen quam fortitudinis habet.[1]

So, throughout the Middle Ages, the element of service to the common weal is inseparable from the idea of magnanimity. And as the word comes into common use among the schoolmen, so it also acquires something of the Christian meaning of virtue in its widest sense.

In the tenth century the Latin word, in this expanded Christian sense, is applied to King Alfred in the chronicles of Ethelwerd:

> A.D. 901. Denique in eodem anno, magnanimus transiit de mundo Aelfredus rex, Saxonum immobilis Occidentalium postis, vir justitia plenus, acer in armis, sermone doctus, divinis quippe super omnia documentis imbutus.[2]

It is interesting to note here the association of justice and *wisdom* with the idea of magnanimity – an association which was to become increasingly important during the Renaissance. That magnanimity is thought of as a Christian virtue is emphasized when we notice that the character of Alfred is summed up more than once by his earliest biographers in terms of the four cardinal virtues. Florence of Worcester, in the early twelfth century, writes of him as 'prudentia, fortitudine, justitia, temperantia praeditus'.

[1] J.-P. Migne, *Patrologiae Cursus Completus*, CLXXI, 1026. ('This courage, since it makes a man prepared to undertake difficulties, strives rather for the common good than for a personal one. For just as knowledge, divorced from justice, is to be called cunning rather than wisdom, so courage, eager for dangers, if inspired by self-seeking and not the common good, may be called rashness rather than fortitude.')

[2] *Monumenta Historica Britannica*, 1848, p. 519. ('Lastly in the same year the magnanimous King Alfred passed from this world, the unshakeable pillar of the West Saxons, a man full of justice, valiant in arms, wise in speech, learned above all in holy scriptures.')

These are learned writers. But in popular use the word becomes associated with a general idea of heroic virtue and thus, by its application to particular heroes, is modified still further. The most famous of all these medieval heroes is Alexander of Macedon, about whom legends cluster as they did about Charlemagne or Arthur. Moralists and theologians alike blamed him for his pride and his incontinence, but his character and his exploits caught the popular imagination, and he became the theme of a number of romances in which the magnanimous Alexander is extolled especially for his personal courage, his liberality, and his love of women. So to the Aristotelian virtue with its Christian accretions are added the specific virtues of the military hero – his capacity to inspire his followers and his readiness in rewarding them, and (in the great age of *amour courtois*) his readiness to lay all these gifts at the feet of love. The prudence of Aristotle was unable to compete in the popular imagination with the dazzling attraction of Alexander. The grand gesture catches the eye.

So, in some of the earliest English usages of the word, magnanimity is often equated with a fiery daring which is very far from Aristotelian in character, and which was in fact reprehended by him as 'foolhardiness' – the 'extreme' of courage. It is of physical courage that Lydgate speaks when he incites Henry VI to imitate the virtues of the Nine Worthies, including 'Alysaundres magnanymyte'.[1] In his *Mumming at London*[2] he associates magnanimity both with *fortitudo* and magnificence, using them almost as interchangeable terms. He first presents Fortune, who is followed

[1] Ballade to King Henry VI Upon His Coronation, *Minor Poems*, E.E.T.S., No. 192, II, p. 627.
[2] Ibid., p. 682. Dr. Ethel Seaton in her *Sir Richard Roos*, 1961, attributes the authorship of this poem to Roos, not Lydgate.

soon after by four ladies 'which shal hir power overgoone' –
Dame Prudence, Dame Rightwysnesse, Dame Fortitudo,
and Dame Feyre and Wyse Attemperaunce. Dame Fortitudo
is very closely related to Aristotle's Magnanimous Man; but
she is also called Magnificence, and she will undertake
dangerous enterprises 'of verray magnanymyte'. Like the
Magnanimous Man she is steadfastly indifferent to all the
changes of fortune, and her power is chiefly used to 'mayn-
teyne the goode comune':

> . . . Sheo of no thing is aferd.
> For comune profit also she,
> Of verray magnanymyte,
> Thinges gret doothe vnderfonge[1],
> Taking enpryses[2], wheeche beon stronge[3].
> And mooste she doothe hir power preove
> A communaltee for to releeve,
> Namely upon a grounde of trouthe;
> Thanne in hir ther is no slouthe
> For to maynteyne the goode comune.
> And alle thassautes[4] of fortune,
> Of verray stidfastnesse of thought
> Alle hir chaunges she sette at nought.
> For this vertu magnyfycence
> Thorough hir mighty excellence
> She armed theos philosophres oolde,
> Of worldely thing that they nought tolde[5] . . .

Magnificence, here rather casually equated with magnanimity, was used in the *Ethics* for another virtue – the extension of liberality to the service of the state. Open-handedness
towards his followers was obviously a highly desirable
quality in a feudal warrior; thus 'magnificence' comes to be

[1] undertake.   [2] enterprises.   [3] dangerous.
[4] the assaults.   [5] valued.

used indifferently either for magnanimity itself or for that quality of liberality which is inherent in it. So Chaucer celebrates it in the *Invocacio ad Mariam:*

> Assembled is in thee magnificence,
> With mercy, goodnesse, and with switch pitee,
> That thou, that art the sonne of excellence,
> Nat oonly helpest hem that preyen thee,
> But often tyme, of thy benygnytee,
> Ful frely, er that men thyn help biseche,
> Thou goost biforn and art hir lyves leche.[1]

The interchangeable terms are becoming less precise, but they are also gaining in richness. To the formal, rather theoretical, ideal of the Greek philosopher are added the overtones of heroic romance and of Christian feeling. The steadfastness of magnanimity, which is a minor consideration in Aristotle, has already a suggestion of Christian feeling in the *Mumming at London;* and by Chaucer it is specifically integrated with Christian theology. It suggests the vigour of the active and asserted will by which the soul may be saved from 'accidie' or 'wanhope' (words expressive of a defeated abandonment to spiritual despair, for which there is no adequate modern translation) which would otherwise swallow it:

> *Fortitudo:* . . . hath manye speces, and the firste is cleped magnanimitee, that is to seyn greet corage; for certes ther bihoveth greet corage agains accidie lest that it ne swolwe the soule by the synne of sorwe, or destroye it by wanhope. This vertu maketh folk to undertake harde thynges and grevouse thynges by hir owene wil, wisely and resonably.[2]

The interchangeability of the two terms becomes increasingly evident, for magnanimity, the inclusive virtue, is here

---

[1] *Second Nun's Tale.*   [2] *Parson's Tale,* 730.

regarded as an attribute of that fortitude which was origin-
ally inherent in it. Again it appears in an exclusively
Christian sense in the *Second Nun's Tale* of Saint Cecilia:

> And right as men may in the hevene see
> The sonne, and moone, and sterres, every weye,
> Right so men goostly in this mayden free
> Syen of feith the magnanymytee,
> And eek the cleernesse hool of sapience,
> And sondry werkes brighte of excellence (ll. 107–12).

Again, as in Ethelwerd's chronicle, one notices the
association of 'sapience' with magnanimity. It is a virtue of
the enlightened understanding; brute courage is not enough.

By the sixteenth century 'magnificence' and 'magnanimity' have become at times synonymous. Spenser's
prefatory letter to *The Faerie Queene* translates Aristotle's
megalopsychia as 'magnificence'. Both words are very fluid in
use, although there is always one constant in the meaning
of each; both imply generosity and an aptness for great and
heroic deeds. Sir Thomas Elyot had been interested in both
words. His dictionary[1] includes

> Magnificentia, a disposicion and administracion in dooing or
> makyng of greate thynges and sumptuous;

and a whole chapter of *The Governour* (1531) is devoted to an
analysis of magnanimity which, rather surprisingly, he
regards as a comparative newcomer to the language. It is

> a companyon of fortitude. . . . It is an excellencie of mynde
> concernynge thynges of great importaunce or estimation,
> doynge all thynge that is vertuous for the achieuynge of
> honour (III, xiv).

As the word is 'yet straunge, as late borowed out of the

---

[1] *Bibliotheca Eliotae*, pub. Thomas Berthelet, 1545.

latyne', he translates it also as 'good courage'. He means by it also the ability to accept adversity and to despise many of the things valued in this world. He who has it practises

> those thynges nat only which be great and moste profitable, but also them which be very difficile, and full of labour and perylle, as well concernynge mannes lyfe as many other thynges there unto pertaynynge.

But beyond this inevitable element of generous courage, the word by the end of the sixteenth century has acquired a great variety of significance according to its context. In casual usage it could have almost the modern limitation of forbearance towards enemies. In 1577, when Sir Philip Sidney refused to speak to Lord Ormond, whom he suspected of prejudicing the Queen against his father, Edward Waterhouse reported that

> the Earl of Ormond saith he will accept no quarrels from a gentleman that is bound by nature to defend his father's causes, and who is otherwise furnished with so many virtues, as he knows Mr Philip to be; and on the other side Mr Philip hath gone as far and showed as much magnanimity as is convenient.[1]

An observer less an admirer of Mr Philip might have felt that it was the Earl who showed the greater magnanimity; but it is the characteristic of such a virtue to beget its own likeness in another.

Shakespeare, in serious vein, uses it (though rarely) solely of valour in arms:

> Methinks a woman of this valiant spirit
> Should, if a coward heard her speak these words,
> Infuse his breast with magnanimity,
> And make him, naked, foil a man at arms
>   (*3 H.VI*, V iv 41–45).

[1] Quoted by Mona Wilson, *Sir Philip Sidney*, p. 75 (1931).

23

But there are a number of times when he gives it ironical emphasis, as when Achilles invites Hector

> to procure safe-conduct for his person of the magnanimous and most illustrious six-or-seven-times-honoured captain-general of the Grecian army, Agamemnon . . . (*T. & C.*, III iii 227).

The 'magnificent Armado' uses it in one of his most delightful pomposities:

> The magnanimous and most illustrate king Cophetua set eye upon the most pernicious and indubitable beggar, Zenelophon (*L.L.L.*, IV i 65).

Falstaff commends 'courageous Feeble':

> Thou wilt be as valiant as the wrathful dove, or most magnanimous mouse (*2 H.IV*, III ii 171),

although his mockery is given the lie when Feeble proves the only one of the pressed recruits who does not try to buy himself out. He 'will ne'er bear a base mind. . . . No man's too good to serve's Prince'. Most interesting of all is Fluellen's dissertation on 'Alexander the Pig', with its obvious parody of learned definitions such as Elyot's:

> Why, I pray you, is not pig, great? The pig, or the great, or the mighty, or the huge, or the magnanimous, are all one reckonings, save the phrase is a little variations (*H.V.*, IV vii 18).

This surely suggests that the word held in such reverence by scholars and courtiers can seem to the ordinary man a little precious and inflated, a balloon that asks to be pricked. Throughout the English Renaissance, however, it is accorded a more than Aristotelian respect by serious moral writers. For them it means more than courage. It is Christian virtue in its widest sense, amounting to a passion for the good life. That very popular sixteenth-century 'courtesy book', *The Institucion of a Gentleman*, is wholly concerned with such virtue; and here it exists chiefly in relation to the good of others:

> A Gentleman shoulde alwaies be armed with fortitude or strength of the mynde, called otherwise Magnanimitie, and to take his profession to be this A defender of right, a soldier of iustice, bearyng with hym a shylde to put away wronges, not only shewed to hymself, but forasmuch as in hym lyeth to defende the ryght of others.[1]

Here again, as in the life of Alfred, magnanimity is specifically associated with the four cardinal virtues necessary to a Christian.[2] Bacon would go still further. He regards magnanimity as that quality of divinity in man by which he is raised above the beasts, and, indeed, transported beyond his own human capacity:

> They that deny a God, destroy Man's nobility: for certainly Man is of kinn to the Beast by his Body; and if he be not of kinn to God by his Spirit, he is a base, ignoble Creature. It destroys likewise Magnanimity, and the raising of humane Nature: for take an example of a Dogg, and mark what a generosity and courage he will put on, when he finds himself maintained by a Man, who to him is instead of a God, or Melior Natura. Which courage is manifestly such, as that Creature without that confidence of a better Nature than his own could never attain. So Man, when he resteth and assureth

---

[1] *The Institucion of a Gentleman*, D iiii (1555).

[2] 'Strengthe of Mynde . . . is one of the iiii cardinall vertues, called *Fortitudo*, asmuch too say, strengthe of thee mind called also noblesse, whiche ought at all tymes to bee founde in noble menne, and suche as descende of noble bloude.'

himself upon Divine protection and favour, gathereth a force
and faith which human Nature in itself could not attain.[1]

One cannot, however, lay too much stress upon the
limitation of a word in any particular context. Wherever it
occurs it is likely that its full range of meaning is at least
latent in the mind of writer and reader alike. It will be
employed most richly by those to whom the concept means
most. When it embodies a great part of the aspiration of two
centuries it will appear most luminously in the work of
those epic writers whose chief theme it is – Spenser and
Milton. In their hands magnanimity sums up the spiritual
greatness of the Renaissance. That it should imply courage,
nobility, and liberality of spirit, is taken for granted by
Spenser. But it is more than this – not only honour itself, but
the passionate desire for honour which is the flame of all his
poetry:

> Yet braue ensample of long passed daies,
> In which trew honour yee may fashioned see,
> To like desire of honour may ye raise,
> And fill your mind with magnanimitee.[2]

Milton uses it in all its apparent senses, of courage, noble
ambition, courageous sacrifice, forbearance and generosity.
But above all, it is the sum of Christian greatness. He uses it,
as Bacon does, for an ambition which is divinely inspired
and sustained; magnanimity derives ultimately from man's
relationship with God, that divine power of self-knowing,
of God-ward aspiration, which confers the right of government over other creatures just in so far as man acknowledges
his own creaturely estate – that of one who may

---

[1] *Essays*, Of Atheism.
[2] *Dedicatory Sonnets*, To the Earl of Cumberland.

> erect
> His Stature, and upright with Front serene
> Govern the rest, self-knowing, and from thence
> Magnanimous to correspond with Heav'n,
> But grateful to acknowledge whence his good
> Descends.[1]

This brief verbal study of 'magnanimity' is merely a sign-post to that which the word embodies. We have now to seek for the concept itself, as far as it may be discovered both in literature and in action.

[1] *Paradise Lost*, VII, 511–16.

Chapter Two

VERTUOUS NOBLESSE

Magnanimity was to become an attribute of heroes in medieval and Renaissance literature; but it was no part of the heroic character in earlier epic poetry. It needed the touch of warmth and grace to bring it to perfection. Beowulf inhabits too bitter a world. He kindles and tends a tiny flame of human loyalty and civilization, flickering in the darkness in the cold winds from a northern sea. His qualities are those of physical courage and endurance, of pride in heroic achievement, moved perhaps by a Christian ideal of self-sacrifice as well as by the demands of tribal loyalty. But in his final parting we feel only the austere dignity of an older and more barbaric world:

> I have ruled this people for fifty years. There was no people's king among the nations about who durst come against me with swords, or oppress me with dread. I have lived the appointed span in my land, guarded well my portion, contrived no crafty attacks, nor sworn many oaths unjustly. Stricken with mortal wounds, I can rejoice in all this.[1]

The words ring harsh for all their greatness. Beowulf is high in honour and rightly proud of his achievements; yet he lacks that final touch of grace which invests those for whom honour is not only the mainspring, the end, the crown of thought and action, but also the highest of all cultivated arts.

The hero of the twelfth-century *Chanson de Roland* is portrayed in warmer colour. There is high tragedy in his

[1] Trans. R. K. Gordon, Everyman, p. 61.

story, and his death is a splendid gesture. Moreover, it is no longer the solitary exploit of the older heroic age, but one shared with his peers. The knightly figure begins to emerge, and the sense of loyalty to a chivalric code as well as loyalty to one's chief. But the latent savagery of the story still divides it from the courtliness of magnanimity.

For, fundamentally, the magnanimous man is also the courtly man. His virtue is not merely innate; it is self-conscious, deliberately cultivated in the midst of courts. It is more sophisticated and complex than mere brute courage. That is why we find no trace of it in some of the earlier medieval romances. Either their subject-matter belonged to an earlier and more barbaric period, or the romances were intended for a wider and more popular audience who would have little appreciation of the niceties of an aristocratic code.

The heroes of *King Horn* (the earliest of the extant heroic tales in English verse, composed in the late thirteenth century), or of the slightly later *Havelok the Dane* and *Guy of Warwick*, are Germanic in type. Strength and physical courage are their chief qualities, and fighting their most important activity. Richard Cœur de Lion would seem to be more promising material. But the fourteenth-century verse romance which celebrates his exploits presents him as a grotesquely violent figure – one who eats the boiled heads of Saracens, and presents some of them, with grisly humour, to an embassy from Saladin. This Richard is nearer to the bogy with whom Saracen mothers threatened their naughty children than he is to the magnanimous man.

One figure, however, caught the imagination of the age and became the mirror in which it saw the qualities it most admired. Alexander the Great was the hero of at least three romances which were immensely popular in their own day – the verse *Life of Alisaunder*, belonging to the end of the thirteenth century; the Scottish *Alexander Buik* and the prose *Life of Alexander*, both of which followed very soon afterwards. Here we find the first literary beginnings of the concept of magnanimity, its first deliberate realization in narrative. The 'exempla' of the period condemn Alexander for his pride and vainglory. But the piety of preachers was not strong enough to destroy the fascination and splendour of so great a conqueror, and in the romances he comes into his own. A bustling and warlike age saw in him all that spelt true greatness.

Alexander's rightful pride and trust in his own ability reflect very closely the Aristotelian *megalopsychia*; but here also is the first indication that Christian humility is beginning to merge with the original concept to create a more gracious figure. He gravely rebukes Darius for his scornful message:

> Thare-fore thare schulde no man that es sett in hye degre triste to mekill[1] in his hyeness, that, thurgh pride and vayne glorye, he schulde despyse the dedis of other men lesse than he.[2]

Nor will Alexander risk the sin of *hybris* in the moment of victory:

> Alexander, if alle he hade the victorye of his enemys, he bare hym neuer the hiere thare-fore, ne empridede hym not thareof. Bot bathe Percyenes[3] & the Macedoyns that ware slaen, he gert brynge to beryell.[4] [5]

He is a man of high personal courage; it is he who sets the example of crossing the bridge of boats and logs which his 'knights' are afraid to pass. But his courage, unlike Richard's,

[1] trust too much.
[2] *Life of Alexander*, E.E.T.S., No. 143, p. 23.
[3] Persians.   [4] caused to be buried.   [5] Ibid., p. 28.

is tempered with generosity: he spares the life of the brave Persian who tries to kill him for the love of Darius' daughter; and towards the dying Darius himself, treacherously murdered by his own servants, he behaves with compassion and fine courtesy. The grand romantic gesture is his also: when he and his army are tormented with thirst, he refuses the one small supply of water, disdaining to be the only one of his host to be so relieved. Interestingly, also, he shows signs of that respect for wisdom and learning which was so much a characteristic of the later Renaissance hero. He never forgets that Aristotle was his tutor; and when he successfully besieges Athens he asks for no other tribute than the provision of ten philosophers to teach him.

But if Alexander of Macedon is the first subject of the literary treatment of magnanimity, he had his counterpart in the contemporary world of action. The ideal could not have flourished so vigorously had it not related to a conscious social aspiration. The magnanimous man in literature is the inevitable correlative of the magnanimous man in the living world.

We have never far to look for the living man. It may be King Alfred – 'vir justitia plenus, acer in armis, sermone doctus' – whose life Milton considered as a possible subject great enough for his projected epic. We may find it in such men as William Marshal who, fighting for his master Henry II against the rebellious Richard, slew Richard's horse in a skirmish, but refrained from following up his advantage against the Prince himself. Richard, on Henry's death, repaid magnanimous courtesy with equal magnanimity, receiving William Marshal into his own service and treating him with honour. Or in the contemporary chronicles of the Crusades, in the pages of Villehardouin and de Joinville, we read of episodes that might have come straight from the romances. De Joinville accompanied St Louis to the Crusades in 1248, about fifty years before the verse *Life of Alisaunder* was written; and in his narrative of actual events we see the same generous respect for honour which characterizes much of the Alexander story. There is the moment when, wounded and surrounded by Saracens, he is in desperate need of help:

> My lord Everard of Sivercy said to me: 'Lord, if you think that neither I nor my heirs will incur reproach therein, I will go and fetch you help from the Count of Anjou, whom I see in the midst of yonder field.' And I said to him: 'My Lord Everard, meseems that you would earn for yourself great honour if you went for help to save our lives; and your own life too is in great jeopardy.' And I spake sooth, for he died of that wound. He sought counsel of all the knights that were there, and all advised as I had advised. When he heard this, he asked me to let go of his horse, which I held by the bridle with the others[1] (p. 191).

De Joinville himself makes a gesture of extravagant chivalry when he has forbidden his sergeants to flee from the Saracens:

> And they said to me: 'Lord, the game is not equal between us; for if it comes to flight, you are on horseback, while we are on foot; and the Saracens will kill us.' And I said to them: 'Lords, I swear to you that I will not fly, for I will remain with you on foot.' So I dismounted, and sent away my horse to the Templars, who were a full crossbow shot behind (p. 280).

Most moving of all is de Joinville's refusal of the opportunity to return home when at last he is released from his long and savage imprisonment in Saracen hands; for he remembers

[1] *Histoire et Chronique du tres Chretien roi Saint-Louis*, trans. Sir Frank Marsials, Everyman.

the words of his cousin-german, the Lord of Bourlement, before they left France:

> No knight, be he poor or be he rich, can come back without dishonour if he leaves in the hands of the Saracens the meaner folk of our Lord, in whose company he went forth (p. 240).

De Joinville's motives would have been understood and respected by his peers in his own generation, many of whom placed honour above the claims of self-interest. These men lived magnanimously; and many of them were fully conscious of the attempt to impose upon real life the pattern of the ideal. St Louis himself distinguishes sharply between the man of mere physical courage (*preux-homme*) and the truly magnanimous man (*prud'homme*) whose honour is founded upon God:

> Il a grant différence entre *preu home* et *preudome*. Car il a mainz preus homes chevaliers en la terre des crestiens et des Sarrazins, qui onques ne crurent Dieu ne sa Mere. Dont je vous di, fist-il, que Dieu donne grant don et grant grace au chevalier crestien que il seuffre estre vaillant de cors, et que il seuffre en son service en li gardant de pechié mortel; et celi qui ainsi se demeine doit l'on appeler *preudome*, pour ce que ceste processe li vient dou don Dieu. Et ceus de cui j'ai avant parlei puet l'on appeler *preuz homes*, pour ce que il sont preu de lour cors, et ne doutent Dieu ne pechié.[1]

[1] de Joinville, *Histoire de Saint Louis*, ed. M. Natalis de Wailly, Paris, 1874. ('There is a great difference between a brave man – *preux-homme* – and a magnanimous man – *prud'homme*. For there are many brave knights in the world, both Christian and Saracen, who have no faith in God nor His Mother. So I tell you (said he) that God bestows a great gift and high grace upon the Christian knight whom He permits to be valiant of body and grants that he may serve Him, while keeping him from mortal sin; and he who thus bears himself may be called a magnanimous man, because his prowess comes to him as a gift from God. And the former of whom I spoke may be called brave men, because they have physical courage, yet fear neither God nor sin.')

St Louis would indeed carry his conception of the *prud'-homme* even further than most of his contemporaries. For them, the ideal operated only within the boundaries of Christendom, and it was generally accepted that a Christian need not respect an oath made to the heathen Saracen. No contract with the enemies of Christ could be considered valid. But

> the holy king so loved truth that . . . he would never consent to lie to the Saracens as to any convenant that he had made with them (p. 139),

a scruple which seemed to surprise even a man of such integrity as his biographer. Sainte-Beuve finely sums up the thought of St Louis in his *Causeries de Lundi:*

> The word *prud'homme* was dear to Saint Louis. . . . He made it comprise, in the sense which he ascribed to it, courage and wisdom, all the qualities of a Christian and an honourable gentleman; he even opposed it to the idea of a rigid piety. It was his cherished ideal for emulation. *Prud'homme* was therefore for Joinville and Saint Louis what the 'beautiful' and the 'good' were to the Greeks, that which was implied by the phrase *honnête homme* in the seventeenth century, a comprehensive and adaptable word which constantly recurs and in which one could imply everything that was finest. De Joinville's *Memoirs*, in the narrative passages, are not so much precise records as a manual and a code of *prud'homie* according to the sainted king. . . .
>
> The word *prud'homie* embraced all the virtues, wisdom, discretion, courage, the spiritual exercise of faith, social responsibility and good manners, as they were understood by that race of ancient Christians, of whom de Joinville is for us the most exquisite flower; and one would best describe this friend of Saint Louis, who in his old age remained so young of heart and so fresh in his memories, by saying that he was

himself the most gracious and attractive of the *prud'hommes* of old time.[1]

In a period when, despite all its cruelties and crudities, the chivalric ideal is such a living force operating upon conduct – even though it may be fully implemented only by the few rare spirits of the age – it is natural that even a classical hero such as Alexander should be presented within the framework of medieval knighthood. Lydgate's *Troy Book* (1412–20) carries the process still further. The 'matter of Troy' is here wholly fused with the contemporary ideals of chivalry, and finds fullest expression in the portrait of the peerless Hector:

> worthy Ector, of knyghthod spring & welle,
> Flour of manhod, of strengthe pereles,
> Crop & rote, grounde of chiualrie,
> Of cher demure, and of curtesye
> He was example – there-to of sobirnes
> A verray merour, & for his gentilnes
> In his tyme the moste renomed,
> To reknen al, and of goodlyhed
> The moste famus. . . .
> And ther-with-al so wys and avysee[2],
> The lowliest eke of his degre
> To riche & pore, and of wordis fewe.
> Vnto alle suche chere he koude schewe,
> Of his presence that glad was euery wight,
> Whan thei at leyser hadde of him a sight;
> He was so benygne to hem of the toun,
> And to his enmyes lyk a fers lyoun
> He koude hym schewe, whan it was to do;
> And in the felde ther myghte no man so,
> To rekene al his labour, half endure (ll. 4802 *seq.*).

[1] Tome VIII (Paris, 1855). My translation.   [2] discreet.

Here are united both the pagan and the Christian qualities of magnanimity – high courage and great strength, courtesy and sober self-control, 'demure' and gentle bearing to rich and poor alike, discretion and wisdom, fierceness to enemies, 'benignity' at home. It is a complete and admirable picture of the medieval ideal, although expressed in conventional terms.

It is left to a more sophisticated poet to give the picture life, individuality, and grace. Hector is caught for ever in the arrested pose of a knight woven in tapestry; but Chaucer's people are as lively, as varied, sometimes as unpredictable, as reality. In the green summer of his world there is an almost infinite lavishness, which seems itself an aspect of magnificence. His poetry is like the landscape he describes:

> a floury grene wente
> Ful thikke of gras, ful softe and sweete,
> With floures fele[1], faire under feete,
> And litel used, hit semed thus:
> For bothe Flora and Zephirus,
> They two that make floures growe,
> Had mad hir dwellyng ther, I trowe,
> For hit was oon to be-holde,
> As though the erthe envye wolde
> To be gayer than the heven,
> To have mo floures sithes seven
> As in the welkne sterres be.
> Hit had forgete the povertee
> That wynter, through his colde morwes,
> Had made hit suffren, and his sorwes,
> Al was for-geten, and that was sene,
> For al the wode was waxen grene;
> Swetnesse of dewe hadde mad it waxe.[2]

[1] many. [2] *The Dethe of Blaunche the Duchesse*, ll. 397–414.

His bounty, like Antony's, has no winter in it. He makes us free of a kingdom; but wherever we travel in it we find one assumption current throughout. Tacitly or explicitly it is taken for granted that 'vertuous noblesse' is the ideal of the best of mankind – an ideal stressed as much by the brutish Miller's lack of it as by the Knight's dedication to it. Chaucer has room for all men in his vast human comedy. He enjoys most and reprobates few. But in the last instance he is always an aristocrat, both in manners and ethics.

Chaucer's poems contain little of the high-heroic of contemporary romances; and unlike Malory and Spenser, who are more profoundly concerned with the philosophy of the good life, he makes no full-scale attempt to portray the magnanimous man in his wholeness. The Knight may certainly seem such an ideal character; yet his portrait, however attractive, is no more than a brief compendium of the conventionally accepted knightly virtues. Here and there in some of the poems we may find some lovely illustration of one of the qualities closely linked with the idea of magnanimity – the idealized humility of Griselda, or the chastity and faithfulness of Constance. His most elaborate analysis of character is the superb study of Troilus as a courtly lover, but this again shows the magnanimous man in one relationship only. Yet implicit within every poem is a criterion which, just because it is taken for granted, indicates a common ideal. This very unselfconsciousness is perhaps more to be trusted as the index to an age than are the more elaborate structures of later writers upon the same theme. Naturally enough it is in the Knight that Chaucer comes nearest to a complete statement of the ideal; and one notices that by now the original Aristotelian *megalopsychia* has blended with Christian concepts of the good life, and thereby acquired an added graciousness. Pagan courage is matched with gentleness. Truth and honour, the attributes of good men in all ages, are allied with medieval 'freedom' – that blend of innate good breeding with generous nobility. And all are crowned with courtesy, more especially the courtesy of abstention from slanderous speech. We are already on the borders of that country in which Spenser's Sir Calidore is to pursue the Blatant Beast, the destroyer of good fame.

Throughout *The Knight's Tale* magnanimity is the commonly accepted standard, apparent even in the very flouting of it at the beginning of the story when Theseus, Duke of Athens, refuses to accept ransom for his two young prisoners, Palamon and Arcite. (This is the same Theseus as he of *A Midsummer Night's Dream*, but a far less sympathetic figure.) Tacitly he is tried and found wanting, for 'pitee renneth soone in gentil herte' and mercy is an essential of greatness. He thus transgresses both the contemporary code of warfare, and the courtly code of 'noblesse', even though he later retracts his harshness.

His prisoners are more truly magnanimous, and this is the quality which governs their oath of friendship that

> never, for to dyen in the peyne,
> Til that deeth departe shal us tweyne,
> Neither of us in love to hyndre oother,
> Ne in noon other cas, my leeve brother,
> But that thou sholdest trewely forthren me
> In every cas, as I shal forthren thee.
> This was thyn ooth, and myn also certein (ll. 1133–9).

Friendship at this level was possible only to persons of 'noblesse' and was still, following Plato, a masculine prerogative. It could be founded only on a spiritual greatness of which the churl could have no conception and of which women were supposed incapable. Even in the days of 'the Most High, Mightie, and Magnificent Empresse Elizabeth', Sidney's Arcadian princesses excel rather in love than in friendship. But love proves too strong for these young knights also. Their friendship is riven by their common love for Emily, whom they view from their prison window; and when they first meet after their escape from prison they prepare to meet in mortal combat for her sake. But in the courtesy they extend to each other even at this moment they once again display their magnanimity:

> Everich of hem heelpe for to armen oother,
> As frendly as he were his owene brother (ll. 1651–2)

Yet the ethic which controls all this formal beauty of behaviour remains only implicit, so much a part of the normal pattern that it calls for no exposition.

The Canterbury Tales, however, contain perhaps the most beautiful of all medieval studies in magnanimity, even though the word itself is never used. Significantly, it is in a story told by a man of substance and position, but one who is not himself of the nobility – the Franklin. He is sufficiently near that charmed circle to be familiar with its values, sufficiently removed to regard them as the object of a distant aspiration, sufficiently *courtois* in his own instincts and desires to be in love with their beauty. The Knight and the Squire could accept them without thought, as a man accepts the familiar furniture of the house which he inhabits; but to the Franklin they are the object of delighted contemplation.

His story gains some of its beauty, as many commentators have noticed, from its position within the whole framework of *The Canterbury Tales*, as the culmination of the 'marriage group'. The Wife of Bath has introduced the series with a description of her own marital experiences, which seem to have belonged to the stock humour of mankind since time began – those of the bullying wife with the hen-pecked husband. She deals with them with a boisterous vigour which, by making all the characters a little larger and a little cruder than life, takes them outside the possible bounds of sympathy. They are safe objects for ridicule, but they leave us with no very ideal conception of marriage; and the angry jesting of the Friar and the Summoner, which immediately follows, can hardly lower the tone any further. The Clerk's voice breaking in, suave and delicately absurd, tries to redress the balance. But we have merely exchanged the world of the cartoon for the world of the fairy story. Griselda, still patient while her husband tests her obedience by one monstrous trial after another, evokes our smiles, our forbearance, even at times our tears; but she is no more a part of the real medieval world than is the fairy beldame of *The Wife of Bath's Tale*.[1] One wishes the same might be said of *The Merchant's Tale* of January and May; but the harsh satire which exaggerates the ugly buffoonery of the betrayed marriage only emphasizes its basis in personal experience.

The Squire's Tale is admirably placed if, as seems likely, it was intended to follow here. The young man of breeding knew how to relieve the embarrassment of the company in the face of this shocking self-revelation. Without appearing

[1] The longsuffering wife is indeed a recurrent figure in medieval stories. Chaucer's own Constance (*The Man of Law's Tale*) has affinities with Griselda, and it seems likely that he also knew of the Flemish St Godeleva, the martyred and murdered wife (cf. Dr M. E. Seaton's article on "Goode Lief My Wife" in *The Modern Language Review*, vol. xli, no. 2, April 1946). But there is an ironic reserve in Chaucer's handling of the theme, which suggests lip-service to the impossible rather than passionate delight in an ideal such as informs the story of Dorigen.

to change the subject too abruptly he can modulate it into a different key, with his elaborate story of courtly love, magic and marvels, and romantic grief. Yet we remain unsatisfied, for we have been faced with a dilemma which remains unresolved. On the one hand is the ethic of courtly love, the lady's absolute dominion over her 'servant'; on the other, the medieval institution of marriage, the husband's lordship over his wife's person, property, and actions. There is too harsh a dichotomy. It outrages dignity that upon marriage the lady should so wholly abdicate her sovereignty; yet that she should retain it outrages decorum and natural law. But here to reconcile these opposing claims comes one of the most gracious stories of the medieval world, *The Franklin's Tale*.

Arveragus and his young wife, Dorigen, begin their marriage with a contract of mutual complaisance, of courtesy and confident trust, which glows like an unwavering flame at the heart of the story. He will serve her in marriage as he did in courtship,

> Save that the name of soveraynetee,
> That wolde he have, for shame of his degree (ll. 751–2).

She for her part will never take advantage of his abdication of lordship, but will remain his 'humble, trewe wyf'.

> Thus hath she take hir husband and hir lord, –
> Servant in love, and lord in mariage (ll. 792–3).

So their days pass 'in blisse and in solas' until Arveragus, pricked by knightly ambition, goes forth 'to seke in armes worship and honour', leaving a heartsick wife to watch the terrible coast which threatens his safe return. Time passes; and the young squire, Aurelius, who for long has worshipped Dorigen with all the fervour of a courtly lover, now casts himself at her feet and prays for grace and pity. But Dorigen is bound by love and her husband's faithful service as well as by marriage. She is wholly her husband's, until Aurelius can remove the hungry rocks which she so dreads. The word is spoken 'in pley' to soften all unkindness in her reply; we lose nothing of the irony by which such courtesy and honour become a two-edged sword against her. For Aurelius, nothing daunted, finds a 'Briton clerk' well skilled in necromancy, pledges the greater part of his patrimony to have the rocks made invisible, and returns to claim his lady's grace. It is at this juncture that Arveragus comes home and discovers his wife's predicament. Here then is a very pretty complication of honours, to be solved only by the most exquisite tact. Arveragus, heart-broken, will yield his own and his wife's honour in order to save her pledge:

> I had wel lever y-stiked for to be,
> For verray love which that I to yow have,
> But if ye sholde your trouthe kepe and save (ll. 1476–8).

Dorigen at his bidding goes to keep her promise 'half as she were mad', so 'looth hir was to been a wikked wyf'. But the squire also is capable of the superb gesture:

> Fro his lust yet were him levere abyde,
> Than doon so heigh a cherlyssh wrecchednesse
> Agayns franchise and alle gentillesse (ll. 1152–4).

The sorrow of his parting and the pride of his 'gentillesse' almost deserve that lovely medieval word 'solempne'; there is something of fine ceremony in his withdrawal, the joyful seriousness of one who partakes in a ritual demanded by high custom. But alas for Aurelius, who must have neither his desire nor his patrimony; he still owes his thousand pounds of pure gold. Already, however, we guess the end, for this magnificent courtesy is catching. The 'philosophre' hears all the story, and touches his own moment of greatness:

> This philosophre answerde, 'Leeve brother,
> Everich of yow did gentilly til other;
> Thou art a squier, and he is a knyght,
> But God forbede, for his blisful myght,
> But if a clerk koude doon a gentil dede,
> As wel as any of yow, it is no drede.
> Sire, I releese thee thy thousand pound (ll. 1607–13).

The Franklin has come to his final challenge. Whether or not he would use the word itself, his story is of the finest flower of magnanimity. All its qualities are there – the great courtesy, the liberality, the pity that runs soon in gentle heart, the passionate dedication to honour. It is a code begotten in courts, but can it be confined to them only?

> Lordynges, this questioun wolde I aske now,
> Which was the mooste fre, as thynketh yow? (ll. 1621–2).

The fragment breaks off here, so that we have none of the pilgrims' comments on the story. But surely the Knight would have been the first to reply with yet another of the great medieval commonplaces, that gentleness is a quality of manners, not birth. *The Wife of Bath's Tale* is concerned with nothing else. The fairy, disguised as a beldame, lectures her unwilling husband upon the subject all through the night:

> But for ye speken of swich gentillesse
> As is descended out of old richesse,
> That therfore sholden ye be gentil men,
> Swich arrogance is nat worth a hen.
> Looke, who that is moost vertuous alway,
> Pryvee, and apert, and moost entendeth ay
> To do the gentil dedes that he kan,

Taak hym for the grettest gentil man.
Crist wole we clayme of hym oure gentillesse,
Nat of oure eldres for hire old richesse;
For, thogh they yeve us al hir heritage,—
For which we clayme to been of heigh parage,—
Yet may they nat biquethe for no thyng,
To noon of us, hir vertuous lyvyng,
That made hem gentil men y-called be (ll. 1109–23).

Magnanimity is of the heart and should be recognized wherever it occurs. The lady should pity faithful service even if her lover is a 'povre bachelor' of low degree (though in the romances he never is, whatever the lowly guise in which he may first appear[1]). The courtly code itself concedes that he may be of low estate, the 'gentle ungentle'. But in actual fact good manners are a great part of magnanimity. Issuing in every appearance of natural grace, they are none the less most carefully cultivated – 'Fredom, and al that longeth to that art'. Such manners spring from the natural sensitiveness of the man of breeding and are not easily learned outside a court. They are the manners of the Man in Black in *The Dethe of Blaunche the Duchesse* who, rudely disturbed from his trance of grief, and seeing that the intruder is his inferior, apologizes charmingly for his abstraction lest the newcomer should be hurt:

Lo! how goodly spak this knyght,
As hit hadde been a-nother wyght.
He made hit nouther tough ne queynte (ll. 528–30).

[1] Nor can I discover any historical instance of a man of low birth winning his spurs. It was indeed possible for one of very modest origins to acquire greatness: William Marshal, born the fourth son of a minor baron, married the rich heiress Isabel, daughter of the Earl of Pembroke, and for nineteen months after the death of King John was regent of England. But the aspirant for knighthood and honour seems always to have had at least some claim to gentle blood.

Whatever the theory, the magnanimous man and the aristocratic man tend to be one and the same; Chaucer makes no conscious distinction between magnanimity and 'noblesse'.

Here then are the common assumptions of the Middle Ages. To see those assumptions most fully integrated into the ideal picture we must turn to the fifteenth-century *Morte Darthur* of Sir Thomas Malory.

Chapter Three

THE DREAM OF SIR THOMAS MALORY

The general reader's conception of medieval chivalry is largely drawn from one man's vision of it when chivalry itself was dead or dying. Chaucer's knight was still an integral part of the world whose needs he answered; he belonged to an order in which magnanimity had been truly enshrined. Malory's King Arthur is a dream of a world now past, recreated in imagination amid the cruder realities of a changed society.

The order of knighthood first arose from the Germanic practice of investing a young man with his arms when he was of age to bear them. Initially, the ceremony was simple enough and had at first no sense of religious significance; nor was the honour dependent on noble birth, although in itself it conveyed social status. In theory at least, and sometimes in practice, a man was knighted for his worth and courage, irrespective of his parentage. In the earlier Middle Ages

> nobility had only two roots: property, by which man entered into a set of relationships determining his place in society; and knighthood, by which he assumed responsibilities and privileges denied to those outside the ranks of the fraternity. The property relationship was born in the act of homage; the knightly relationship in the act of initiation to knighthood. The first gave a man a place in a hierarchy; the second in a brotherhood.[1]

The brotherhood was international, and acknowledged no

[1] R. W. Southern, *The Making of the Middle Ages*, 1953, p. 111.

other claims to status beyond its own code. But gradually that which had begun as a social group convenient to a warring society was transformed into an order with religious sanctions, and acquired an almost mystical aura. The growing menace of the Muslim world united the order of chivalry as the champion of Christianity against 'hethenesse', and St Bernard's call to the Crusades created the ideal of a knighthood wholly dedicated to the service of religion. The Hospitallers of St John of Jerusalem were founded about 1099; and about 1118 Hugh de Payens founded the Knights Templars (Pauperes Commilitones Christi templique Salamonis), who were specifically enjoined to follow as nearly as possible the rule of St Augustine.

The ceremony of investiture acquired a religious symbolism as it became more elaborate. Two accounts[1] of the initiation of the Knights of the Bath give us a full description of it.

The squire aspiring to knighthood, having served the king with one course at dinner, and dined himself, is then shaved and goes to the bath, which is covered by a linen cloth. While he is in the bath the lords and knights give him his charge:

> He must love God, be steadfast in the faith, uphold the Church, and be true to his sovereign and his word. He must also uphold widows in their rights, and succour them and maidens with his goods if required. He must not sit in any place where judgment is wrongfully given, but must as far as in his power bring all murderers and extortioners to justice.

The knights then make a cross on the aspirant's shoulder

[1] (a) A thirteenth-century French poem, L'Ordene de Chevalerie. (b) Nicholas Upton, De Studio militari (in the reign of Henry VI). For this description I am indebted to the Cambridge Mediaeval History, VI, xxiv, from which I quote.

with water from the bath, kiss it, and wish him 'worship' in the name of God. He is laid in bed, arises and dons a hermit's garments, and keeps a night vigil in the chapel. In the morning he confesses and hears Mass, and offers a taper with a penny in it. He is then reclothed in his knightly garments, and invested with his spurs and sword in the presence of the king, who kisses him and bids him be a good knight.

The significance of all this elaborate ceremony is carefully explained. The young squire comes from his bath as free from sin as the babe at the font. By knighthood he should be led to win a bed in Paradise. His scarlet gown shows that he must be ready to shed his blood in the service of God and his Church, and the white belt that he must keep his body pure.[1]

This elaborate ceremonial has moved far from the early simplicity with which knights had once been created, often on the field of battle. But it reflects the combination of romance and religion which gave the ideal of chivalry its attraction and its semi-sacred associations.

[1] Is it the picture of this initiation ceremony and its religious symbolism which inspires the lovely fifteenth-century lyric?—

> He bare him up, he bare him down,
> He bare him into an orchard brown.
>
> In that orchard there was an halle,
> That was hanged with purpill and pall.
>
> And in that hall there was a bede,
> It was hanged with gold so rede.
>
> And in that bed there lithe a knight,
> His woundes bleding day and night.
>
> By that bede side kneleth a may,
> And she wepeth both night and day.
>
> And by that bede side there stondeth a stone,
> *Corpus Christi* wreten there on.

Chambers and Sidgwick, *Early English Lyrics*, LXXXI.

There were undoubtedly those, such as St Louis of France, to whom the virtues of the *prud'homme* were a very real ideal by which to live, and there were many who deserved the reverence in which knighthood was at one time held. But many things combined to its final decay. The men of a violent and rapacious age failed to implement ideals so high. The fall of the Knights Templars in 1312 was the scandal of chivalry, whether or not the charges of corruption and heresy were in all respects justified. The sheer cost of horse and armour made knighthood possible only to those of wealth and power, while the weight of his equipment made the knight less effective in the field than the more lightly armed troops who began to replace him. The development of other weapons, too – the longbow and gunpowder – made him of less value as a fighting unit; and the numbers of the nobility had in actual fact been decreased by a century of warfare and civil strife. In the fifteenth century there are knights still existing (of whom Sir Thomas Malory himself was one), but they have become decorative anachronisms rather than the champions of Christendom. Caxton's own lament interpolated in *The Order of Chivalry* reflects the sad consciousness of change:

O ye knyghtes of Englond, where is the custome and vsage of noble chiualry that was vsed in tho dayes? What do ye now but go to the baynes and playe atte dyse? And some not wel advysed vse not honest and good rule, ageyn alle ordre of knyghthode. Leue this, leue it, and rede the noble volumes of Saynt Graal, of Lancelot, of Galaad, of Trystram, of Perseforest, of Percyual, of Gawayn and many mo. There shalle ye see manhode, curtosye and gentylnesse.[1]

This translation of a fourteenth-century French prose work

[1] *The Order of Chivalry*, Kelmscott Press, 1893, p. 99.

restates the ideals of knighthood as they were conceived at their highest:

> God of glory hath chosen knyghtes by cause that by force of armes they vaynquyshe the mescreauntes, whiche daily laboure for to destroye holy chirche. . . . Thoffyce of a knyght is to maynteyne and deffende his lord worldly or terryen, for a kyng ne no hyhe baron hath no power to mayntene ryghtwysnesse in his men without ayde and helpe. . . . By the Knyghtes ought to be mayntened and kept justyce. . . . Thoffyce of a knyght is to mayntene and deffende wymmen, wydowes & orphanes, and men dyseased and not puyssaunt ne stronge . . . to have a castel and horse for to kepe the wayes & for to deffende them that labouren the londes and the erthe . . . also to enserche for theves, robbours and other wikked folk, for to make them to be punysshed. . . . Justice, wysedom charitie, loyalte, verite, humylite, strength, hope, swiftnes and al other vertues semblable, apperteyne to a Knyght. . . . Lyke as God hath gyven to hym an herte to thende that he be hardy by his noblesse so ought he to have in his herte mercy, and that his courage be enclyned to the werkes of myserycorde & of pyte. . . . Thenne yf thou wylt fynde noblesse of courage, demaunde it of faythe, hope, charyte, justyce, strengthe, attemperaunce, loyaulte, and of other noble vertues, for in them is noblesse of courage.[1]

This analysis of the knight's character into the three theological virtues of faith, hope, and charity, and the four cardinal virtues of justice, prudence, strength, and temperance, may seem to divorce him wholly from the classical pattern of magnanimity. But the last four, combined with physical courage, are as Aristotelian as they are Christian. Yet when we turn from this recreation of a past ideal to the ideal itself as it appears in Chaucer, we are conscious of a certain inconsistency. Can it be that Chaucer's knights,

[1] Ibid., pp. 19-44.

delightfully romantic as they are, are yet presented with a touch of satire? The attitudes of Palamon and Arcite, though splendid and wholly proper, are none the less ever so slightly absurd. The faint echo of mockery is that reserved for real life, for institutions sufficiently secure to withstand the assaults of humour. Both Caxton and Malory, however, are wholly serious in their manner – it has the solemnity of threnody. Their lovely iridescent bubble might break against the edge of laughter.

For Malory's is indeed a world of dream, even though he is engaged on the apparently prosaic task of translating a 'French book' in which the *Morte* itself is only one of a number of stories with different heroes, all members of the Round Table. This change of focus from book to book adds to the sense of an enchanted and fantastic world. Amid these green forests of remote kingdoms, the sunlight and the banners and the spears, the brilliantly coloured pavilions, stories slip mysteriously into one another, knights pass and reappear or are wholly lost. But most readers are content to accept the unexplained, to be carried forward with the flow of pageantry and the rhythmic enchantment of words. There is flux in that world, but no bewilderment, for the theme of all the stories is one. The whole, as Malory presents it, is an intricate study of the pattern of 'noblesse' or magnanimity.

Not even Spenser has studied it with more passion or more subtlety; and certainly Spenser had no such intractable material to subdue. For Malory lives between two worlds. The earlier magnanimous hero, whether the pagan Alexander or the Christian Arveragus, followed a straight course; the ideals of his class and time were accepted without question. Spenser's heroes were in a faery land where, to some extent, they create their own ideals. But the knights of the *Morte Darthur*, for all their marvellous adventures, represent the highest of a real but passing world in an age which has begun to question its values. Galahad and Launcelot are types of magnanimity indeed, but magnanimity measured by two mutually exclusive standards, which Professor Vinaver would call those of Carbonek or Camelot – the fortress of the Christian soul or the palace of courtly love. Malory is always conscious of both; and it is the conflict of the two, each so lovely and beloved, which haunts the very rhythms of the *Morte Darthur* like the echo of a passing-bell.

If we look for the traditional values of magnanimity they are easy enough to find. In Sir Palomides or Sir Lamorak there is even something of the austere simplicity of Roland; the glory of the personal exploit is for them an end in itself. It is even an echo of that earlier period that Sir Palomides, the Saracen knight, is sometimes represented as less noble in his means of achieving the prise than are his Christian opponents. Liberality, another traditional element, is a part of King Arthur's virtues as it was of Alexander's. After the battle with the eleven kings, Merlin exhorts him to reward his followers freely:

> Rewarde youre good knyghtes with golde and with sylver, for they have well deserved hit. There may no ryches be to dere for them, for of so fewe men as ye have there was never men dud more worshipfully in proues than ye have done today (I, p. 37).

As the feudal relationship of the lord to his followers is made plain here, so is the converse displayed in the many instances of generous loyalty either to the king or to the one from whom knighthood has been received. Sir Gareth defends Sir Launcelot even against King Arthur:

Also kynge Arthure blamed sir Gareth because he leffte hys felyship and hylde with sir Launcelot.

'My lorde,' seyde sir Garethe, 'he made me knyght, and whan I saw hym so hard bestad, methought hit was my worshyp to helpe hym. For I saw hym do so muche dedis of armys, and so many noble knyghtes ayenste hym, that whan I undirstode that he was sir Launcelot du Lake I shamed to se so many good knyghtes ayenst hym alone.'

'Now, truly,' seyde kynge Arthur unto sir Gareth, 'ye say well, and worshypfully have ye done, and to youreselff grete worshyp. And all the dayes of my lyff,' seyde kynge Arthure unto sir Gareth, 'wyte you well I shall love you and truste you the more better (III, p. 1114).

So also Sir Gareth refuses to join the conspiracy against Launcelot, 'for I shall never say evyll by that man that made me knyght'.

This is a world apparently simple and uncomplicated, which the writers of the earlier medieval romances would have understood, just as they would have accepted the *amour courtois* of Tristram for La Beale Isoud or of Launcelot for Guenevere. It is the world of the grand gesture: Sir Blamore having vowed to suffer death rather than yield to Sir Tristram, Sir Tristram himself entreats for his life; or Sir Lamorak and Sir Tristram, after long and valorous combat, wish each to yield to the other that he 'may have the worship of this battle'. Most moving of all is the occasion in one of the last tragic battles in which the fellowship of the Round Table crumbles to its end, when Sir Launcelot comes to the aid of the king:

And ever was kynge Arthur aboute sir Launcelot to have slayne hym, and ever sir Launcelot suffird hym and wolde nat stryke agayne. So sir Bors encountirde wyth kynge Arthur, and sir Bors smote hym, and so he alyght and drew hys swerde and seyd to sir Launcelot,

'Sir, shall I make an ende of thys warre?' (For he mente to have slayne him.)

'Nat so hardy,' seyde sir Launcelot, 'uppon payne of thy hede, that thou touch hym no more! For I woll never se that moste noble kynge that made me knyght nother slayne nor shamed.'

And therewithall sir Launcelot alyght of hys horse and toke up the kynge and horsed hym agayne, and seyd thus:

'My lorde the kynge, for Goddis love, stynte thys stryff, for ye gette here no worshyp and I wolde do myne utteraunce. But allwayes I forbeare you, and ye nor none off youres forberyth nat me. And therefore, my lorde, I pray you remembir what I have done in many placis, and now am I evyll rewarded.'

So whan kynge Arthur was on horsebak he loked on sir Launcelot; than the teerys braste oute of hys yen, thynkyng of the grete curtesy that was in sir Launcelot more than in ony other man. And therewith the kynge rod hys way and myght no lenger beholde hym, saiyng to hymselff, 'Alas, alas, that ever yet thys warre began!' (III, p. 1192).

Personal courage, liberality, loyalty, love, generosity of heart – all these are a part of magnanimity, yet they can occur even in a materialist's conception of chivalry. But constantly intruding upon all this, contradicting it, conflicting with it, ultimately destroying it, is a wholly different world, the world of the Christian mystic.

It is odd that so eminent an authority as Professor Vinaver should consider Malory as a materialist, one who 'took a sceptical view of the supernatural'. It is true that in his version of the *Morte* he reduces the element of the marvellous. But the mystic is not necessarily one who believes in marvels: there can hardly be anything more practical and fundamental than the direct experience of God which the mystic is always seeking – an experience in which the

marvellous, although it may sometimes occur, is accidental
and irrelevant. And here it is that Malory excels. There are
few moments which so subdue the reader to awe and worship as those in which he describes the final vision of the
Sangreal, the chalice of the Last Supper, relying on no
other marvel than the familiar symbol of the sacrament:

> Than loked they and saw a man com oute of the holy vessell
> that had all the sygnes of the Passion of Jesu Cryste bledynge all
> opynly, and seyde,
>
> 'My knyghtes and my servauntes, and my trew chyldren
> which bene com oute of dedly lyff into the spiritual lyff, I woll
> no lenger cover me frome you, but ye shall se now a parte of
> my secretes and of my hydde thynges. Now holdith and
> resseyvith the hyghe order and mete whych ye have so much
> desired' (II, p. 1030).

and again, when the long quest of Sir Galahad is finally
achieved:

> He called sir Galahad unto hym and seyde,
>
> 'Com forthe, the servaunte of Jesu Cryste, and thou shalt se
> that thou hast much desired to se.'
>
> And than he began to tremble ryght harde whan the dedly
> fleysh began to beholde the spirituall thynges. Than he
> hylde up his hondis towarde heyvn and seyde,
>
> 'Lorde, I thanke The, for now I se that that hath be my
> desire many a day. Now, my Blessed Lorde, I wold nat lyve in
> this wrecched worlde no lenger, if hit myght please The,
> Lorde' (II, p. 1034).

The mirror of chivalry and the mirror of Christ: it seems
at first as if they could reflect the same world without
distortion. The Christian virtues of humility and holy
courtesy appear at times to be assimilated with ease into the
chivalric code. The greatest knights are the first to ascribe
'worship' to one another:

'I take God to recorde,' [says Sir Launcelot] I never was wrothe nor gretly hevy wyth no good knyght and I saw hym besy and aboute to wyn worshyp; and glad was I ever whan I founde a good knyght that myght onythynge endure me on horsebak and on fote (III, p. 1198).

But yet each knight is on fire for his own personal glory, however noble and selfless the deeds he performs as a means to it. The humility of knighthood is a gracious and ennobling virtue, but it shines with a different light from that of God. As long as the story is measured by the standard of chivalry, its splendour is undimmed. But from the moment that Galahad, the Christ-type, appears, the colours begin to change. The pageantry is rich as ever, but over it fall the first shadows of the destined end, subduing the sunlit brilliance to the sombreness of dusk. At the heart of it glows the steady radiance of the Grail, but beyond the fringes of that light the darkness presses in. The change comes upon us slowly. The first shadow is but the faintest, transitory dimming of the light, in the foreboding of Sir Launcelot as he gazes at the miraculous sword in the stone:

So whan the kynge had sene the lettirs he seyde unto sir Launcelot,
'Fayre sir, thys swerde ought to be youres, for I am sure ye be the beste knyght of the worlde.'
Than sir Launcelot answerde full sobirly,
'Sir, that ys nat my swerde; also, I have no hardines to sette my honde thereto, for hit longeth nat to hange be my syde. Also, who that assayth to take hit and faylith of that swerde, he shall resseyve a wounde by that swerde that he shall nat be longe hole aftir' (II, p. 856).

The two realms, of knighthood and the spirit, have been glimpsed for a moment side by side; and the one that has hitherto seemed so solid begins to lose its firm outline in the glittering and dissolving light shed by that other radiance. Again and again the values of chivalry and courtly love are brought to the test by such a juxtaposition, and every time they are reversed. It is when Launcelot is most aware of himself as a 'synful man' that he comes nearest to spiritual power. When Sir Urre seeks the healing that can be effected by none 'untyll the beste knyght of the worlde had serched hys woundis', Launcelot protests almost with anguish against making the attempt. Being commanded by King Arthur himself, he dare not disobey,

> 'but and I myght or durste, wyte you well I wolde nat take uppon me to towche that wounded knyght in that entente that I shulde passe all othir knyghtes. Jesu deffende me from that shame' (III, p. 1151).

Sir Urre is healed according to Sir Launcelot's prayer, 'by the grete vertue and grace of The, but, Good Lorde, never of myselff'; but, while the whole court gives thanks, 'ever sir Launcelot wepte, as he had bene a chylde that had bene beatyn'.

'Of all knyghtes sir Launcelot bearyth the floure', and Sir Ector's great lament for him is a lament for all chivalry:

> 'Thou sir Launcelot, there thou lyest, that thou were never matched of erthely knyghtes hande. And thou were the curtest knyght that ever bare shelde! And thou were the truest frende to thy lover that ever bestrade hors, and thou were the trewest lover of a synful man that ever loved woman, and thou were the kyndest man that ever strake with swerde. And thou were the godelyest persone that ever cam emonge prees of knyghtes, and thou was the mekest man and the jentyllest that ever ete in halle emong ladyes, and thou were the sternest knyght to thy mortal foo that ever put spere in the reeste' (III, p. 1259).

But again and again in the last books of the *Morte Darthur* the same phrase echoes on the ear. He is the best of 'ony synfull man of the worlde'; but the magnanimity of knighthood is not alone enough. It yields to the greater magnanimity of Christ's 'true servant', and Launcelot gives place to Galahad.

The courtesy and humility of the courtly lover are founded on a false premise. Malory rejects them with grief, for they were lovely in themselves; but his judgement is unshaken. Its dreadful finality is apparent less in the fact of the parting of the two great lovers, than in the barrenness of that parting. After all its length of years, all its adventures, all its griefs and triumphs, so great a love can bring no final trust:

'The selff desteny that ye have tekyn you to, I woll take me to, for the pleasure of Jesu, and ever for you I caste me specially to pray.'

'A, sir Launcelot, if ye woll do and holde thy promyse! But I may never beleve you,' seyde the quene, 'but that ye woll turne to the worlde agayne.'

Their parting, at least, might have been one perfect act; but a bitter word has blighted it. And the last moment of farewell is one of sterile frustration:

'Wherefore, madame, I praye you kysse me, and never no more.'

'Nay,' said the quene, 'that shal I never do, but absteyne you from all such werkes' (III, p. 1253).

Because so many readers tend to regard this parting as the tragic climax of the book, we are apt to relegate King Arthur himself to second place. Yet it is doubtful whether Malory would have intended it so. For, when he wrote, the Arthurian tradition was still growing in popularity rather than declining. For at least 200 years Arthur had been celebrated as one of the Nine Worthies, where Caxton also gives him his due place:

> Now let us thenne remembre what hysteryes ben wreton of cristen men, of whom ther be many wreton. But in especial, as for the best and worthyest, I fynde fyrst the gloryous, most excellent in his tyme, and fyrst founder of the round table, Kyng Arthur, Kyng of the Brytons, that tyme regnyng in this royaume. . . . But thystorye of the sayd Arthur is so gloryous and shynyng, that he is stalled in the fyrst place of the mooste noble, beste and worthyest of the cristen men.[1]

The tradition is as lively as ever in Elizabeth's time, so that Spenser does nothing new in choosing him as the pattern of magnanimity. It is hardly likely that Malory would do less reverence to this 'gloryous and shynyng' figure. Fewer adventures are recorded of the king himself than of his knights; but in nearly every story it is Arthur who is the begetter of glory, both the incentive of valour and its rewarder. The fellowship of the Round Table is bound together by the honour of the king. And if we study Arthur himself the magnanimous pattern emerges in its entirety, divested of the spiritual paradox which makes Launcelot but a distorting mirror of its truth. The king has the personal courage, the liberality, the innate courtesy to high and low, the discretion and truthfulness, which form so great a part of the magnanimous ideal. Above all he reconciles mercy and loyalty with justice.

The long struggle that King Arthur makes to trust his wife and his friend proceeds from no mere moral muddle. It springs directly from the Christian element of magnanimity. His personal humility and loyalty constrain him to trust as long as trust is possible, that he may never impugn

[1] *The History of Godefrey of Boloyne and of the Conquest of Iherusalem*, Kelmscott Press, 1893 (Preface).

'worship' where it is deserved; and discretion and reason restrain anger. When he receives the slanderous letter from King Mark his generosity of spirit shames in our eyes the malice of the sender.

> Whan kynge Arthur undirstode the lettir, he mused of many thynges, and thought of his systyrs wordys, quene Morgan le Fay, that she had seyde betwyxte quene Gwenyver and sir Launcelot, and in his thought he studyed a grete whyle. Than he bethought hym agayne how his owne sistir was his enemy, and that she hated the quene and sir Launcelot to the deth, and so he put that all oute of his thought (II, p. 617).

If he were not in the seat of judgement he would himself do battle for his queen's honour.[1] But when at last the proof of guilt is beyond all doubt, he addresses himself to justice. Though the queen is still fair and beloved and Launcelot the best knight of the world, Arthur accepts the tragic destiny which places the duty and honour of the king above that of lover and friend. He alone of the great protagonists remains true both to the world of chivalry and the world of the spirit, and the final elegy of the *Morte Darthur* is not that uttered by Sir Ector for Sir Launcelot, but by Sir Launcelot himself after the burial of the queen:

> 'for my sorow was not, nor is not, for ony rejoycyng of synne, but my sorow may never have ende. For whan I remembre of hir beaulté and of hir noblesse, that was bothe wyth hyr kyng and wyth hyr, so whan I sawe his corps and hir corps so lye togyders, truly myn herte wolde not serve to susteyne my careful body. Also whan I remembre me how by my defaute and myn orgule and my pryde that they were bothe layed ful lowe, that were pereles that ever was lyvyng of Cristen people, wyt you wel,' sayd sir Launcelot, 'this remembred, of

[1] III, 1050.

their kyndenes and myn unkyndenes, sanke so to myn herte that I myght not susteyne myself' (III, p. 1256).

As the last light flickers over Camelot, the ideal is vindicated. Magnanimity is no longer merely the *megalopsychia* of the Aristotelian hero, nor the magnificence of chivalry. It is the nobility of the Christian knight arrayed in the whole armour of God. False knights in the stories yet to come may fight against God; but the magnanimous man fights for Him.

Chapter Four

THAT MOST HEROICKE SPIRIT

For many generations men still awaited the return of Arthur, and kept alive the spirit of his greatness. Simple folk, and perhaps some others, cherished at least a half belief in his actual reappearance at the time of England's need. He and his knights were ceremonially recalled at court functions for two or three hundred years. Thomas Milles in his *Catologue of Honour* (1610) recalls that William de Montacute earl of Salisbury, 'died at the Iusts and Turneys at Windsore, upon the Friday being the 30. of Ianuary, the 18. of *Edward* the third, 1343, at what time King Edward did celebrate the solemnity of the Round Table'; and the tradition of the tournament was still continued by Elizabeth, chiefly as an occasion for pageantry and display.[1]

In Elizabethan England the Arthurian tradition was strengthened both by a strong national consciousness which made Arthur the symbol of English dominion, and by the growth among scholars of antiquarian interests. The cult showed itself in various ways. There was even in London a company of archers calling themselves the 'Knights of Prince Arthur's Round Table'. The title of Prince rather than King was probably in compliment to Henry VII's eldest son, who was renowned for his skill in archery. This

[1] Such occasions are celebrated in Peele's *Polyhymnia*, which describes the tournament before Elizabeth on 17 November 1590 (the anniversary of her accession), and are delightfully and intimately recalled by William Higford in his *Institutions, or Advice to His Grandson*. See Chapter VII of this book.

young man, the first Tudor to be proclaimed Prince of Wales, was no doubt so christened to strengthen the Tudor myth that in their line Arthur himself had returned to his native throne. The courtly world hailed Elizabeth as Arthur's descendant and inheritor of his honour. Even later, when Jonson presented his *Masque of Oberon* to Prince Henry in 1611, the same tradition is still invoked:

> This is a night of greatnesse, and of state;
> Not to be mixt with light and skipping sport:
> A night of homage to the *British* court,
> And ceremony, due to ARTHURS chaire.[1]

The tradition of bygone glory is thus invoked to give lustre to the present, and it is natural enough that Arthur should become Spenser's pattern of Magnificence. But in the long, bright dream of *The Faerie Queene* it is tempting for the modern reader to imagine that his magnanimity is a literary concept only, the elegy of a dead past. Yet, only three years before the appearance of Spenser's poem, died one who proved that it was not a dream at all, but the image of that which men might still pursue as an attainable ideal. In 1586 Sir Philip Sidney,

> that most heroicke spirit
> The hevens pride, the glory of our daies,[2]

died of a gangrenous wound, but 'left the vivid air signed with his honour'.

In the anguish of those last days Sidney wished to destroy his *Arcadia*. But, had we so lost it, we should have lost the greater part of the evidence as to why Sidney was the darling of his age, the pattern of all honour, his death the theme of countless elegies, private sorrow, and public lamentations.

[1] *Works*, ed. Herford and Simpson, VII, 352, l. 320.
[2] Spenser, *Dedicatory Sonnet to the Countess of Pembroke.*

The mere acts of his life are not enough to convince a later generation; other Elizabethans also were young men of valour and promise, others also died greatly. But here within this pastoral, this most fragile and brightly coloured of all the bubbles of the romantic imagination, the ideals by which Sidney himself lived are made explicit.

The plot of the *Arcadia* is no more than the conventional romance popular with most Elizabethan writers. Basilius and Gynecia, the sovereigns of Arcadia, withdrawing into the simplicity of a rural retreat, with their two daughters Pamela and Philoclea, are found by two young princes, Musidorus and Pyrocles. Musidorus, falling in love with Pamela, disguises himself as a woman in order to be near her, but accidentally becomes the object of the Queen's infatuation. Intrigues and distress complicate the story, a revolt of the populace shows how wrong it is in a sovereign to abdicate his responsibilities even for the most idyllic existence (a theme twice used by Shakespeare, in *Measure for Measure* and *The Tempest*); but finally all misunderstandings are resolved, justice is done under the auspices of Evarchus, father of Misidorus, who – as one fully expects in a sixteenth-century romance – fortunately happens to be travelling in Arcadia just when he is most needed, and the pairs of lovers are united.

Merely as a story, it is as complicated and unconvincing as a romance can well be, although the political implications are serious enough, and reflect an author concerned with the practical realities of contemporary experience. But it is less for the story that one reads the *Arcadia* than for its sheer delight in life itself, in the brightness of the world, the charm of youthful love, and the sheer attraction of goodness. For true greatness in Sidney's eternal country (and it has the air of eternity about it) can exist only in the beauty of virtue –

one might almost say in the beauty of holiness – but only the great in birth and breeding are likely to be virtuous in so high a fashion. This sense of the alliance of noble blood with noble conduct was no form of snobbery, but a feeling for the responsibilities imposed by greatness. It was part of the Elizabethan passion for decorum that men of high place, such as Sidney himself, should be fitted for high office and high courtesy. The pomp and state with which Sidney travelled in Europe, the eulogies which his diplomatic service won for him at foreign courts, the great matches tentatively proposed, were but fitting for one whose good birth made him the servant of his country. It was a career undertaken as a matter of course, and largely sustained out of his private purse. The magnanimous man in the days of a powerful baronage had been much concerned with his own personal prowess and prestige. But the Elizabethan magnanimous man is increasingly devoted to the public service of his country. It was an ideal largely encouraged by Elizabeth's treatment of her courtiers. That great and shrewd queen made favourites of few but those who could serve England, and who were willing to spend themselves and their fortunes, often with little enough return. When they ceased to serve well they ceased to be favourites, as Essex discovered to his cost. That Sidney himself takes such service for granted appears in his letter to his brother Robert, about to begin his travels abroad:

> I presume soe well of you, that . . . your purpose is being a Gentleman borne, to furnish your selfe with the knowledge of such thinges, as maie be serviceable to your Countriee, and fitt for your calling (III, p. 124).

So also, in a more bitter mood, he writes to Hubert Languet, the famous scholar who was his friend and mentor, acting when Sidney first knew him as the representative in Paris of the Elector of Saxony:

> I have quite forgotten the use of the pen, and my mind itself – if ever it was of worth – begins imperceptibly and even quite contentedly to grow slack in this ignoble sloth. For what is the use of urging our minds to acquire knowledge unless there is some opportunity of using them for the public good, which in these corrupt times one may not hope for (III, p. 119).[1]

This conscious devotion of great talents to great service is very naturally and properly allied to an Aristotelian awareness of one's own worth. When, at the end of the *Arcadia*, Evarchus yields to the request that he should act as judge, his response might have been that of Sidney himself:

> To this the secrett assurance of his owne worthynes (whiche allthough yt bee never so well clothed in modesty yet allwayes lives in the worthiest myndes) did muche pussh hym foreward: Saying unto hym self, the treasure of those Inward giftes hee had were bestowed by the goddes uppon hym to bee beneficiall, and not Idle (IV, p. 335).

Such an attitude is as far from arrogance as it is from the habitual self-deprecation of our modern world, in which greatness must at all costs be disclaimed or, if furtively acknowledged, regarded as a source of embarrassment. It has only the simple dignity of self-knowledge. The same spirit which accepts and admits its own talents is the cause of a just indignation when it meets with unworthy treatment. So Pamela resents her imprisonment as Shakespeare's Cleopatra does her grief, in a manner 'fitting for a princess descended from so many royal kings':

> But Pamela, allthough indewed with a vertuous myldenes, yet the knowledg of her self and what was due unto her made her

---

[1] My translation from the Latin original.

hart full of stronger disdayne ageanst her adversity. . . . And as in panges of death the stronger hart feeles the greater torment, bycause yt dothe the more resist to his oppressor, so her mynde the Nobler yt was sett and had allredy embraced the higher thoughtes, somuche more yt did repyne (IV, p. 343).

It is the same spirit which prompts Sidney to write to his father-in-law, Sir Francis Walsingham, 'I shall not by other mens wantes be drawn from my self'.

The worth which justifies such claims is not merely that of birth and privilege, or even of an innate disposition to goodness. It is an achievement won of effort and struggle. Sidney can contemplate innocence with reverent delight, but he is as rigorous as Milton in refusing to accord to a 'fugitive and cloistered virtue' the quality of true magnanimity. It is most startlingly apparent in that he denies it to the very heroine whom he has created with such devotion. When Philoclea is first tempted by love we are left in no doubt that simplicity is far from the steadfastness of true magnanimity, even in those innately good:

The sweete mynded *Philoclea* was in theyre degree of well doynge to whome the not knowyng of evell serveth for a grounde of vertue, and holde theyre inwarde powers in better Temper with an unspotted simplicity, then many, who, rather cunningly seeke to knowe, what goodness ys, then willingly to take unto them selves the followyng of it.

True yt ys, that that sweete and symple breathe of heavenly goodnes ys the easyer to falle, bycause yt hathe not passed throughe the worldly wickednes, nor feeling founde the evill that evell carryeth with yt (IV, p. 103).

The truly magnanimous man must, like Sir Guyon, 'see and know, and yet abstain'.

The line of descent still runs true. What we see in the *Arcadia* is a development of Aristotle's *megalopsychia*, not a divergence from it. Its outward and visible sign is still that of physical courage. Cleophila shows herself, alone, to the enraged mob of rebels:

> Truely owtewarde graces are not with owte theyre efficacyes, the goodlynes of her shape, with that quyet Magnanimity represented in her face in this outter moste perill, did even fixe the eyes of this barbarus people with thadmiration uppon her (IV, p. 123).

But this outward manifestation proceeds from an inward nobleness of thought, reflecting like a mirror the nobility of its peers. So Musidorus rebukes Pamela's doubts of his worthiness:

> 'Yow doo wronge to youre self, to make any Doubte that a base estate coulde ever undertake so hye an enterpryse, or a spotted mynde bee ever able to beholde youre vertues (IV, p. 186).

Fulke Greville reminds us that this same exquisite grace of thought was in Sidney himself, so that he found it difficult to entertain even a suspicion of disingenuousness in another. Greville recounts his friend's attempt to join Sir Francis Drake's expedition to the West Indies in 1585. Perplexed and troubled by the frustrations that he met, Sidney was still loath to attribute them to any lack of frankness in Sir Francis:

> After we were laid in bed [I] acquainted him with my observation of the discountenance and depression which appeared in Sir Francis; as if our coming were both beyond his expectation, and desire. Nevertheless that ingenuous spirit of Sir Philip's, though apt to give me credit, yet not to discredit others, made him suspend his own, & labor to change or qualifie my judgement.[1]

[1] Fulke Greville, *Life of Sir Philip Sidney*, ed. Nowell Smith, p. 74.

Are we not reminded of King Arthur, holding King Mark's slanderous letter in his hand, yet disdaining to give it credence? There is a kind of spiritual fastidiousness which becomes increasingly apparent in Elizabethan magnanimity, and which often shows itself in hatred of the mean or paltry. Both Sidney and Spenser use 'coward' and 'cowherd' interchangeably. Probably they did not confuse the two words in origin; but it seems at least probable that an association of idea is deliberately emphasized – to which Harington's phrase, 'base and dunghill dispositions', lends further likelihood. What bitter scorn appears in the description of

> the righte nature of a villeyn, never thincking his estate happy, but when hee ys able to doo hurte (IV, p. 118).

The condemnation of the villain is the same blindness which falls upon those who love darkness rather than light because their deeds are evil. The twisted spirit of Tymantus, who fails to tempt Philanax into treason, can see in his goodness nothing but a reflection of his own baseness – the exact converse of honour which attributes its own virtue to others:

> [He] rather thoughte yt some Further fetche of Philanax (as that hee woulde have all to hym self alone) then was any way taken with the Lovely beuty of his vertue, whose Image hee had so quyte defaced in his owne sowle that hee had lefte hym self no eyes to beholde yt (IV, p. 302).

Baseness is more likely to be found among the base-born; but lowliness in itself is not to be despised. Indeed, it may often be the occasion of a greater courtesy, as it was in Chaucer's Man in Black. We are strongly reminded of him when Evarchus receives a woeful suppliant:

> Evarchus rose up unto hym, with so gracyous a Countenance, as the goodnes of his mynde had longe exercysed hym self unto, carefull so muche more to discend in all Curtesyes as hee

69

sawe hym beare a Lowe representacyon of his afflicted state (IV, p. 333).

We notice once again the emphasis on the fruits of a long discipline; Evarchus 'had long exercysed hym self' in magnanimity. Yet for the supreme gesture of courtesy to the lowly we must go outside the pages of the *Arcadia*, and watch Sidney himself as, mortally wounded, he relinquishes his cup of cold water to the soldier who was 'gastly casting up his eyes at the bottle'. Indeed, there are times when it is hard to distinguish between the Arcadian princes and their creator. As the romance draws to its climax, the lineaments of magnanimity are more and more clearly depicted. In imprisonment and danger the princes touch true greatness; high-hearted and high-thoughted, their untroubled serenity shines with a steadfast flame. They are

lyke a Man that has sett the keeping or leaving of the body as a thinge with oute hym selfe and so thereof had a freed and untrubled Consideracyon (IV, p. 280).

But the same serenity illumines the intimacy of a personal letter from Sidney to his father-in-law. Among the nigh intolerable difficulties which beset him as Governor of Flushing – lack of supplies, of money, of men, of support – he writes to Sir Francis Walsingham:

I had before cast my count of danger want and disgrace, and before God Sir it is trew that in my hart the love of the caws doth so far over ballance them all that with Gods grace thei shall never make me weery of my resolution. . . . For me thinkes I see the great work indeed in hand, against the abusers of the world, wherein it is no greater fault to have confidence in mans power then it is to hastily to despair of Gods work. I think a wyse and constant man ought never to greev whyle he doth plai as a man mai sai his own part truly though others be out but if him self leav his hold becaws other mariners will by ydle he will hardli forgive him self his own fault. For me I can not promis of my own cource . . . becaws I know there is a hyer power that must uphold me or els I shall fall, but certainly I trust, I shall not by other mens wantes be drawn from my self (III, p. 166).

Here indeed is 'the fairest flowre in field that euer grew', as Spenser called him, a man who was himself the living embodiment of the ideal he created for others. There was a daily beauty in his life which touched the imagination of his contemporaries: and when he died they knew that something high and shining had departed with him. He had brought the ideal into contact with daily life and had shown it to be possible fact.

> They that knew him well, will truly confess, this *Arcadia* of his to be, both in form and matter, as much inferior to that unbounded spirit of his, as the industry and Images of other mens works, are many times raised above the writers capacities. . . . His end was not writing, even while he wrote . . . but both his wit and understanding bent upon his heart, to make himself, and others, not in words or opinion, but in life, and action, good and great.[1]

In their admiration of him men paid their own tribute to goodness. It is this which inspires the arrogant humility of the inscription which Sir Fulke Greville devised for his own tomb at Warwick: 'Fulke Greville; Servant to Queen Elizabeth: Councillor to King James: Friend to Sir Philip Sidney.'

Without changing the nature of the traditional values, Sidney had deepened and enriched them. Musidorus and Pyrocles have inherited from Aristotle their physical courage, their firmness of temper amid all the variations of fortune, their liberality, their sense of personal dignity and

[1] Fulke Greville, op. cit., p. 20.

honour. Their courtesy and chivalry, their generosity of spirit, are the legacy of Chaucer and Malory. But fully explicit in the *Arcadia* is a further quality only rarely glimpsed in earlier studies of the magnanimous character – the love of learning and art which became the accepted attribute of the Renaissance gentleman. For the medieval courtier it was enough to excel in chivalry – learning might safely be left to clerks, whose business it was. But the influence of Castiglione, of Elyot, of Ascham, combined with the emerging need for an educated governing class, began to make scholarly attainments a desirable part of a gentleman's education. Fashion, education, intellectual endowment, and his own natural bent, combine to make Sidney himself the pattern of Renaissance culture – student as well as soldier, poet as well as courtier, patron as well as creator. He encourages his brother's studies, corresponds with learned men, gives hospitality to writers with whom he himself can discuss the critical theories of his time.

> The Universities abroad, and at home, accompted him a general *Maecenas* of learning; Dedicated their Books to him; and communicated every Invention, or Improvement of Knowledge with him. . . . His heart, and capacity were so large, that there was not a cunning Painter, a skilfull Enginier, an excellent Musician, or any other Artificer of extraordinary fame, that made not himself known to this famous Spirit, and found him his true friend without hire; and the common *Rende-vous* of Worth in his time.[1]

So Musidorus and Pyrocles, the true mirrors of their creator, travel to attain knowledge, encourage the poetic contests of the Arcadian shepherds, and themselves take part in them. Yet, even without their evidence, the *Arcadia* proclaims itself the creation of a writer to whom the world of honour and

[1] Greville, op. cit., p. 33.

the world of art are one. He praises the loveliness of virtue in words that sing themselves in the heart. High actions are but the outward impression of inward contemplation, reflected in the grave poise of the sentences, their delicate cadences, their words as cool and fresh as water shining in sunlight. Whether he looks inward at the heart of man or outward at the world about him, all that he sees fills him with delight and reverence as the fit subject of knowledge:

> And see you not [says Pyrocles] the rest of all these beutyfull flowers, eche of whiche woulde requyer a mans witt to knowe, and his lyfe to express? (IV, p. 12).

Above all, Sidney's is a Christianized magnanimity. His princes and princesses are assumed to live in a world of classical paganism; they discuss the after-life in the terms of Plato's *Phaedo*; but the basic assumptions of their thought – the famous prayer of Pamela in prison, the innocence of Philoclea, the truth of the two young princes, the discussion on the possible justification of suicide (a possibility finally refuted) – all these are founded on a life-time in the Christian faith.

Here, then, in Sidney himself and his *Arcadia*, magnanimity acquires the greatest depth and extension of meaning that has yet occurred in its history. It comprises the self-knowledge and dignity, the tempered steadfastness, the liberality, the physical courage, of the ancients; the knightly chivalry and the *amour courtois* of the medieval world; the sense of public service, the graciousness and learning of the Renaissance; even the generosity towards enemies which is almost the only meaning retained, in a bloodless and attenuated form, in the twentieth century. For one who lived by such a standard, death by the grand gesture seems but a fitting climax. If Sidney had not thrown away his thigh pieces as a gesture of respect towards the old Lord Marshal, Sir William Pelham, who was unable to wear his because of a recent wound, he would not himself have received his mortal hurt. To a world such as our own, educated to think personal security one of the highest goods, and mediocrity almost a virtue (how often we laud the 'little man'!), such an action must seem futile and extravagant. Yet surely it keeps 'decorum' with all that we know of the man and his work; it has that quality of high romantic grace which made him for a whole generation the embodiment of that which inspired men. And perhaps it is for just such a reckless extravagance that our own more cautious and calculating age is homesick. It is as warming as a fire in a cold room to a generation only too often afraid that there is no cause left to die for.

> My overcoat, like yours, is an Ideal,
> With a gulf for pockets – nothing there to steal
> But my empty hands, that long have lost their use,
> With nothing now to make, or hold, or lose.[1]

All that Sidney stood for can be summed up in the words of Musidorus as, with Pyrocles, he waits in expectation of death:

Wee have lived and have lived to bee good to ourselves, and others, our sowles which are putt into the sturring earthe of our bodyes have atcheved the causes of theyre hether coming, they have knowne and honoured with knowledge the cause of theyre Creation: And for many men (for in this tyme place and Fortune yt ys lawfull for us to speake gloriusly) yt hathe been behovefull that wee shoulde live (IV, p. 344).

It is magnificently and rightly said, and Sidney's own best epitaph.

[1] Edith Sitwell, *Tattered Serenade: Beggar to Shadow*.

Chapter Five

TH'ETERNALL BROOD OF GLORIE

Chaucer, Malory, and Sidney wrote of high things with a high purpose; and Spenser followed their example when, in the prefatory letter to Sir Walter Raleigh which accompanied the first three books of *The Faerie Queene* in January 1589/90, he claimed that his intention was 'to fashion a gentleman or noble person in vertuous and gentle discipline'. The letter has aroused particular interest because of the problem it presents as to the relationship of the poem to the scheme here outlined for it. The apparent inconsistencies between the two have perhaps distracted attention from the wider interest of the whole letter as part of a strong tradition. This indication of the intended framework of his poem serves chiefly to indicate Spenser's ultimate purpose, an end far more important than the means. And that purpose is so true to the literature of the great tradition and so foreign to that of our own century, that it is worth some examination here.

All the writers whose work has so far been discussed in this study would have agreed that the poet or story-teller has one supreme function: by giving delight he is to make his readers fall in love with virtue. Delight, like so many of our older words associated with happiness and festivity (such as 'solempne' or 'pompous'), has a more inward meaning than mere entertainment or passing pleasure. 'Delight,' says Sidney, 'hath a joy in it, either permanent or present. Laughter hath only a scornful tickling.'[1] This is the kind of

[1] *Apologie for Poetry.*

joy which the writer seeks to convey. It is implicit in the triumphant challenge to the hearer's sense of honour with which the Franklin concludes his lovely story: 'Which was the mooste fre, as thynketh yow?' It is an echo in mood of St Paul's exhortation to the Philippians:

> Whatsoever things are true, whatsoever things are honest, whatsoever things are just, whatsoever things are pure, whatsoever things are lovely, whatsoever things are of good report; if there be any virtue, and if there be any praise, think on these things.

By the time of Caxton, the writer's function has become an accepted norm, movingly expressed in the famous Preface to the *Morte Darthur*:

> I have doon sette it in enprynte to the entente that noble men may see and lerne the noble actes of chyvalrye, the jentyle and vertuous dedes that somme knyghtes used in tho dayes . . . humbly bysechyng al noble lordes and ladyes wyth al other estates, of what estate or degree they been of, that shal see and rede in this sayd book and werke, that they take the good and honest actes in their remembraunce, and to folowe the same. . . . Doo after the good and leve the evyl, and it shal brynge you to good fame and renommée.

Elizabethan writers go further. They not only take it for granted that poetry should provide matter for emulation. They elaborate a theory of the means by which it is 'to soften and polish the hard and rough dispositions of men, and to make them capable of virtue and good discipline'. So says Sir John Harington, in the *Briefe Apologie for Poetrie* with which he prefaces his translation of Ariosto's *Orlando Furioso*. Poetry may appear 'in a manner vaine and super-fluous', yet it is by the study of poetry that we may be led to philosophy and even to theology itself.

Therefore do we first read some other authors, making them as it were a looking glasse to the eyes of our minde; and then after we have gathered more strength, we enter into profounder studies of higher mysteries, having first as it were enabled our eyes by long beholding the sunne in a bason of water at last to looke upon the sunne it selfe.

It is perhaps a little difficult not to suspect Harington of special pleading. The *Orlando* was, after all, an offering to his queenly godmother, Elizabeth; and he has also to make out a case for the pagan 'fables and imitations' which so delighted his youthful spirits. He sets the story of Perseus and the Gorgon, for instance, tottering under the weight of allegory upon allegory – the 'Historicall sense' of the story itself; the 'moral allegory' in which the Gorgon represents sin and vice; the 'natural allegory' by which Perseus vindicates man's ascent, by his nature, 'to the understanding of heavenly things, of high things, of eternal things'; the 'heavenly Allegorie' of the soul's dissevering from corruption; and finally the 'Theological Allegorie', by which Perseus represents 'angelicall nature, daughter of the most high God', the divine vice-regent as Nature appeared to the medieval world, 'killing and overcomming all bodily substance'. Ovid's charming story is but a frail foundation for a structure rising to such dizzy heights, and one half suspects the smile with which the young man triumphantly turns back, in conscious virtue, to the pagan pleasures of the *Metamorphoses*. But that more sober genius, Edward Fairfax, makes the same claim, though less elaborately, in his Preface to *Godfrey of Bulloigne* (his translation of Tasso's *Gerusalemme Liberata*) in 1600:

Heroicall Poetrie . . . is compounded of Imitation & Allegorie: with the one she allureth unto her the mindes and eares of men, and maruellously delighteth them; with the other, either in virtue or knowledge, she instructeth them.

And he instances the increase of magnanimity itself as one of the specific ends of poetry.

All this is but an elaboration of Sidney's own famous dictum in his *Apologie* that the poet

doth not only show the way, but giveth so sweet a prospect into the way, as will entice any man to enter into it. . . . With a tale forsooth he cometh unto you, with a tale which holdeth children from play, and old men from the chimney corner. And, pretending no more, doth intend the winning of the mind from wickedness to virtue.

Even Bacon, in his most severely analytical study, would exalt the function of poetry above that of history, for

it appeareth that poesy serveth and conferreth to magnanimity, morality, and to delectation. And therefore it was ever thought to have some participation of divineness, because it doth raise and erect the mind, by submitting the shows of things to the desires of the mind; whereas reason doth buckle and bow the mind unto the nature of things.[1]

The end of poetry then (in which all forms of story-telling are tacitly included) is to breed magnanimity itself, 'th'eternall brood of glorie excellent'. None of these men would have understood the possibility of writing merely to entertain, which would have seemed to them an abrogation of their proper function. Later writers may have been predominantly concerned with man as he is, but those in the heroic tradition were concerned with man as he might and ought to be.

This therefore is the intended function of *The Faerie*

---

[1] *Advancement of Learning*, II iv 3.

Queene, which Spenser elaborates in his prefatory letter to Sir Walter Raleigh. His primary aim is simple, lofty, and traditional. Like Ariosto and Tasso, with whom he deliberately challenges comparison, he intends to present 'a gentleman or noble person in vertuous and gentle discipline', that his readers may be stirred to emulation. The poem is to be an allegory of the moral world. The Faerie Queene herself is a symbol of glory, and Prince Arthur of 'Magnificence' (which, as we have seen, is used interchangeably with 'magnanimity' at this period). So far all seems well. Given Arthur as the patron of Magnificence, which is 'the perfection of all the rest', the general framework of the story – the adventures of successive knights of the Faerie court, each embodying some one of the virtues comprised in magnanimity – is obvious enough. The difficulty for many readers occurs when Spenser relates his structure more specifically to an Aristotelian scheme. Arthur is

> perfected in the twelue priuate morall vertues, as Aristotle hath devised, the which is the purpose of these first twelve books: which if I finde to be well accepted, I may be perhaps encoraged, to frame the other part of polliticke vertues in his person.

Spenser completed only a quarter of his projected epic; but already he has diverged very far from Aristotle, if we are to understand his statement in a rigidly literal sense. His story as far as we have it concerns the patron knights of Holiness, Temperance, Chastity, Friendship, Justice, and Courtesy; while the two *Mutabilitie* cantos suggest that there may also have been intended a knight of Constancy. But no human or faerie champion appears in these two last cantos, and they belong so much more properly to the realm of myth than of allegory, that they seem scarcely relevant to the purpose of the rest of the poem. (Yet one is tempted to wonder whether here Spenser may be setting the scene for the quest of Arthur himself, in the consummation of which the claims of temporal and eternal glory might finally have been reconciled, and mutability past.)

A first glance at this outline of the virtues shows how very far removed Spenser's poem is from the *Ethics*. Aristotle would scarcely have recognized holiness as a virtue at all, had he even grasped its implications. Even to the Christian it is perhaps less a virtue than a way of life. Justice was to Aristotle a political rather than a private virtue. Neither chastity, friendship, nor courtesy comes independently within his discussion of goodness. On these grounds the assumption has sometimes been made that Spenser's letter represents either an original plan from which he had diverged, or a later rationalization which he may have hoped to implement when the poem was finally completed.

It is possible that both suppositions are unnecessary. It is surely likely that 'as Aristotle hath devised' may refer not to the content but to the method of the analysis of virtue. Indeed, to a poet who is writing professedly as a Christian, Aristotelian magnanimity must have seemed wholly inadequate to his vision. The enumeration of its qualities could not, by its very nature, tally with a Christian ideal. Aristotle's magnanimous man is worthy of all respect, but he is still a pagan. He is the best that classical philosophy can devise; but Dante left even the greatest of the pagan philosophers – Plato, Socrates, and Aristotle himself – in Elysium indeed, but within the first circle of Hell. Not baptized into the Christian faith, they are incapable of the full consummation of Christian bliss. Spenser would not have argued with Dante. The framework of the poem is indeed suggested by the *Ethics*; but its virtues are those of the Christian saint, of another order altogether.

The Faerie Queene had, in its own time, an advantage which it has since lost. It assumptions about the spiritual and moral life of man would be shared by all its readers. Allegory is a frigid business if it requires the reader to equate an improbable sequence of events with what seems to him an antiquated and no longer acceptable system of ideas. But when it incarnates in delightful story his own deepest experiences of the spiritual life, it becomes an intellectual adventure of the most exciting kind. For the Christian of any generation as for the readers of its own period, *The Faerie Queene* is an experience which brings his own moral world sharply into focus, and the correspondence of its various planes is the essence of the pleasure which it gives.

The endless ramifications of the story may seem bewildering on a first acquaintance with the poem. The reader finds himself within a sunlit world of grassy plains, of woodlands and waterfalls, of gardens and enchanted palaces. Rather as in the *Morte Darthur*, knights and ladies, giants and dragons, appear, encounter, and disappear again, like the phantasmagoria of dream; and it is tempting to enjoy them as one does a happy dream, yielding uncritically to a series of inconsequent delights. Yet to do so is to look at and admire a banquet and come away unfed. It is not Spenser's fault if we do so. His subject is so vast that he needs the infinite variety of his Faerie Land in which to explore it fully in all its aspects. But he has given us a map of that enchanted world, and it is our fault if we fail to use it.

Readers have often noted that the first book is the most self-contained and most firmly constructed of the whole epic. It is natural that it should be so. For the Red Cross Knight shows us the way across the whole world of Faerie

Land, the journey which every one of the knights must ultimately undertake – the journey from Cleopolis to the Heavenly City.

> Till now, said then the knight, I weened well,
> That great *Cleopolis*, where I have beene,
> In which that fairest *Faerie Queene* doth dwell,
> The fairest Citie was, that might be seene;
> And that bright towre all built of christall cleene,
> *Panthea*, seemd the brightest thing that was:
> But now by proofe all otherwise I weene:
> For this great Citie that does far surpas,
> And this bright Angells towre quite dims that towre of glas
>
> (I x 58).

Red Cross is the only one of all the knights who sees the whole of that ultimate journey as it lies before him; and the road goes across the countryside, as plainly as Christian's, from Elizabethan London to the heavenly Jerusalem. The gates of the bright City do not open for Red Cross, who has still another task to do. But he has entered upon the Christian way of life, fought in its armour, been restored by heavenly grace, and through experience regained the lost innocence of Eden. This is the final labour which every knight must undertake. But where the knight of Holiness shows us the whole journey, the others range to and fro upon the various adventures which are incidental to it.

The plan of the epic, then, is clear enough. With all the charm of romantic adventure, it is to make an anatomy of the virtues, 'as Aristotle hath devised', and to relate them all to the totality of Christian experience. First in the Book of Holiness we are given the essential meaning of the whole, a key to all the subsequent stories. And then, in successive books, we are to be shown that

82

> goodly golden chaine, wherewith yfere
> The vertues linked are in louely wize (I ix 1).

The poem concerns a quest, to which other quests also are incidental. 'Magnificence' is therefore only one part of the story. The other, possibly more important, is the end and purpose of the quest, which is glory. Had the epic been completed, the importance of this end would have been clearer; for the whole poem is working towards the final consummation – Arthur's own quest in which magnanimity meets with glory, and in which perhaps the gates of the shining City will open at last. But from the present fragment of the whole design the reader can only deduce what that glory was meant to be by a study of the quests which were to lead to it.

First we see, firmly and decisively laid down in Book I, the pattern of common Christian experience. Una (Truth) seeks aid for her royal parents, whose kingdom is ravaged by an evil dragon, and Red Cross becomes her champion. Many adventures delay or deter him: he must kill the worm of error, learn to resist the allurements of Duessa or false-seeming, pass through the palace of Pride and the Den of Despair, be instructed in the House of Holiness, and finally overthrow the dragon in a terrible combat which he wins only through the strength and refreshment offered by the Well and Tree of Life. Una's knight is but newly entered upon the Christian life. Never before has he worn the silver armour with the blood-red cross, and he has to vindicate his right to it. Like many a newly instructed Christian, he finds it comparatively easy to defeat intellectual error, but is nevertheless betrayed by doubt in his personal relationships. Success in resisting the temptation of the flesh lays him open to a danger more secret and unrecognized. He trusts too much to his own sense of integrity – perhaps even a little encouraged in his self-confidence by the supposed faithlessness of Una – and so falls at length into the toils of spiritual pride and overweening. Truth herself frees him, by the aid of heavenly grace; but in the first bitter recognition of his own weakness he mistakes remorse for repentance and is barely rescued from despair. But taught at last what true repentance is, by patient and humble submission to the life of Christian discipline, his 'cured conscience' makes him strong enough to encounter the power of hell itself and, refreshed and heartened by heavenly grace beyond his own deserving, to overcome it and to regain as conqueror that state of Eden-innocence which Adam had once lost. Yet it is not the same innocence as Adam's. The innocence of unknowing has the dew of Paradise still upon it; but that reconquered by struggle and experience has a beauty all its own. The one wears the face of childhood, the other that of old age sifted by past griefs and victories. It is not only by accident that the Book of Holiness is followed by that of Temperance which, having full knowledge of evil, can yet abstain.

It is indeed inevitable that Spenser should turn first to temperance or self-control as the first link of the 'goodly golden chaine'. Without such discipline no other virtue is obtainable; and this, of all the others, is the one most clearly common both to Aristotle's scheme, which Spenser wishes to emulate, and the Christian way of life. Throughout the Middle Ages, also, temperance was commonly presented as necessary for continuance in all other forms of goodness. In the *Mumming at London*, as we have seen, Dame Feyre and Wyse Attemperaunce appears with Prudence, Rightwysnesse, and Fortitudo, each of the four sisters being essential to virtue. In Skelton's interlude of *Magnificence*[1],

[1] E.E.T.S., Extra Series, XCVIII.

Measure (moderation) at first orders all things aright within the kingdom until, with his banishment by his extravagantly generous prince, liberty becomes licence and largesse recklessness; but the prince is finally saved by the aid of various allegorical personages (such as Perseverance and Goodhope) of whom Measure himself is the chief. Measure's descent from Aristotle is clear enough, but with the medieval tendency to blur the sharpness of classical thought, the Aristotelian mean has been identified even more especially with self-control:

> For Measure is a meane, nother to hy nor to lowe,
> In whose attemperaunce I haue suche delyght
> That Measure shall neuer departe from my syght.

This interlude, written in the time of Henry VIII, contains the moral commonplaces which must have been a part of Spenser's own education. Thus living Christian experience, the Aristotelian example, and the medieval tradition, make the primacy of Sir Guyon natural. His story is that of the temperate knight whose quest is the overthrow of the wicked enchantress, Acrasia, who destroys her victims through poisoned pleasures and enervating lusts. On his journey he must defeat the unbridled rage of Furor, the lust of Cymochles, and the burning vengeance of his brother Pyrochles. He must resist the material temptations of Mammon, raise the siege of the House of Temperance, and finally destroy Acrasia's Bower of Bliss.

One by one Sir Guyon passes through the common temptations to uncontrolled passions – anger, frivolous desires, cupidity, and lust. But this is no austere ascetic. The strongest impression which he leaves in the mind is that of a burning reality moving amongst shadows – not a negative abstention, but a positive and vital force. It is the evil characters who appear ineffective, starved of all true pleasure, the very satisfactions which they seek being (as Professor C. S. Lewis has stressed in his *Allegory of Love*) mere imitations of reality. The lust of Cymochles, 'like an adder lurking in the weeds', is no more than that of a peeping Tom: Phaedria's idle, tinkling, pointless merriment is as hollow as that laughter which Sidney so despised, which 'hath only a scornful tickling'. And Acrasia herself, in that oppressive garden where metallic leaves betray the living senses, and the birds must tune their voices to the sound of silver instruments and contrived fountains, is quenched like a candle-flame by sunlight when faced suddenly with reality.

This positive and vital strength of Sir Guyon, this weapon of the tempered will, is essential to every knight who would follow the magnanimous quest of glory. Sir Guyon's final victory is over lust and diseased desire; and it is natural that chastity, as the highest form of self-control, should be the subject of the next adventure. Britomart, the maiden knight, has fallen in love with her destined husband, Arthegall, shown to her by Merlin in a magic mirror, and now seeks him through the world. Her quest is not completed in this book, which is unusually complicated by the interaction of other adventures – the flight of Florimell (the perfect beauty pursued by many knights), the creation of a false and soulless Florimell by a witch, the betrayal of Malbecco by his wanton wife. But Britomart's own service is to free her twin sister, Amoret, wife of Sir Scudamore, from the lustful tyranny of the enchanter Busirane. Here is another of Spenser's glorious positives; it is not natural to him to think in terms of mere abstention. His is not a merely physical or sexual chastity, but a delicate reverence towards all created things. Britomart is not merely the adversary of lust: that would have been to duplicate Sir Guyon's victory, and for all his lavishness Spenser is never wasteful. She is the assertion of love against every travesty of itself in whatever form. She encounters the casual wantonness of Malecasta; the self-regarding virginity of Marinell, which also tries to present itself as chastity; the soulless seeming-chastity of the false snow-maiden Florimell; and the outrages of savage lust. Most hideous, most frustrate, and most lewd of all the enemies of chastity which Britomart must meet, is the jealousy which destroys in Malbecco not only love but the last traces of humanity itself. But more significant still, Britomart comes to the rescue even of lawful wedded love. She passes unharmed through the flame which would have destroyed Sir Scudamore, the 'inordinate affection' which, even in faithful marriage, may hinder love's true fruition. True chastity is not self-denial. It is the highest point of human love where it meets with the grace of God.

Just as chastity is the noblest and fullest expression of love between man and woman, so friendship is the noblest expression of love in society. Loyalty is its basis, and the fourth book is concerned with loyalty and truth as much as with the affections of friendship. Because it is a virtue possible only in society, the book has no one distinctive patron. Cambell and Triamond, who are expressly intended to embody the idea of friendship, have only a small part in the narrative, which has a number of interlocking themes, some of them picking up stories from the other books. It contains the discovery of the false Florimell, the witch-created snow-maiden of the previous book, and continues the story of Britomart herself in the long-sought meeting with Sir Arthegall; the real Florimell is at last united with her true lover, and the mythical marriage of Thames and Medway is evocative of the later *Mutabilitie* cantos. The tyranny of the maiden Poeana is overthrown and she learns to keep 'decorum' as a wife; and centrally placed in the book is the famous episode of the disgrace and sorrow of Arthur's squire Timias, by which Spenser sought to reinstate his friend and patron, Sir Walter Raleigh, in the Queen's favour after his ill-starred marriage. But just as the previous book is concerned with love in opposition to all debasements of itself, so this is concerned with the contrast between truth and seeming-truth in human relationships – the test of all real friendship. The false Florimell is carelessly wooed by the false-hearted Blandamore and Paridell; falsely she assumes the golden girdle of her true counterpart; of all knights she chooses the empty Braggadochio. Timias forgets his faith to Belphoebe. Poeana, loving Amyas who rejects her, unwittingly takes the faithful Placidas as her lover; and when Arthur appears to succour the distressed and to reunite lover with lover and friend with friend, he gives reality to a hitherto false relationship when he persuades Placidas to wed Poeana. His most essential function in this book is to act as the touchstone between true and false.

Spenser has shown that friendship without truth is impossible. He goes on to show that there can be no true friendship without a just relationship among men, both as individuals and as members of society. The fifth book of *The Faerie Queene* is concerned with the quest of Britomart's love, Sir Arthegall, the knight of Justice, deputed to rescue Irena, whose lands are wrongfully withheld from her by the wicked Grantorto. Helped by his iron page, Talus, Sir Arthegall performs various acts of justice on the way, but is himself defeated and shamefully enthralled by the Queen of the Amazons (through too strict an adherence to a promise which should never have been made), and is ultimately rescued by Britomart. Thereafter he is received in the palace of Mercilla, where he sees justice dispensed by mercy, before he completes his mission.

Justice, in its most absolute sense, cannot be treated as if it operated separately in private and political life, and part of Book V is necessarily political. But by far the most lively and interesting part of the book is concerned with justice in personal relationships. At first it is closely linked with chastity, true love opposed to lawless lust. Then its victory over bribery and greed recalls the necessity of temperance as the foundation of virtue. Next Sir Arthegall encounters the giant with the scales, who wishes 'all things [to] reduce unto equality'. (Again, as we have so often seen in this poem, the patron 'virtue' finds a travesty of itself among its enemies.) The episode of the giant reminds us urgently that justice is more than human equity, and certainly far other than equality. It is part of a cosmic harmony against which men rebel at their peril, one in which every element of the universe has its appointed place.

> Such heavenly iustice doth among them raine,
> That euery one doe know their certain bound,
> In which they doe these many yeares remaine,
> And mongst them al no change hath yet beene founde.
> But if thou now shouldst weigh them new in pound,
> We are not sure they would so long remaine:
> All change is perillous, and all chaunce vnsound (V ii 36).

This is the kind of universe in which alone Spenser's thesis is valid – an ordered harmony which makes sense of human experience, and in which magnanimity, itself a form of harmony, is a natural ideal. The magnanimous man is one who orders his unruly will and affections in a divinely ordered world. From this consideration of man's just place in the universe, Spenser goes on to consider rightness and decorum in personal relationships. It is beautifully devised that Britomart should herself repeal the Amazon law of female supremacy. The husband who abdicates his position as head derogates from his wife's dignity as well as his own; and it is in the voluntary respect which she accords to her husband that the wife is most truly fulfilled. Justice consists not in mastery but in free consent. It is only when a man's life is securely founded upon the justice of his own personal relationships that he is capable of administering political justice. Arthegall must be released from his outrageous thralldom to the Amazons before he can himself rescue Irena from oppression and fulfil his quest.

Courtesy, following the grave issues with which the poem has so far concerned itself, may seem light in the balance, until Spenser makes us realize its true nature. Only the Christian knight so disciplined in the other qualities of magnanimity – disciplined in the will by temperance, in the heart by chastity, in his personal and social relationships by friendship and justice – is capable of true courtesy, here shown in the story of Sir Calidore, whose task is to subdue the Blatant Beast, destroyer of honour and good fame. As in Book III, the plot is obscured by a number of interlacing stories imposed upon it, although all illustrate the diverse forms of courtesy or its opposite – whether the adventure of the wounded knight and his wife, brutally denied hospitality; the natural grace of the forest-bred youth of noble parentage; the attacks of the Blatant Beast itself; or Coridon's churlish envy of Sir Calidore when, in disguise, he courts the shepherdess Pastorella. The courtesy here shown is a quality of innate reverence, bred in the spirit although expressing itself in manners. It is nourished indeed in courts, but is always native to the gentle-hearted, and we are shown it in all its forms. It is trained and exquisite in Sir Calidore himself; but it is also innate in the noble blood of the forest-born squire, latent even within the savage and untaught when moved with compassion, and to be found innocently unsophisticated among the shepherds. Above all it is a courtesy which not only refrains from scandal and offence, but is actively concerned to sustain another's honour.

Entry on the Christian quest, temperance, chastity, loyalty, justice, courtesy – these things we know are included in Spenser's concept of magnanimity. There is also another knight, Sir Sophy, who is mentioned as being, together with Sir Arthegall, high in the favour of the Faerie Queene. Sidney and Spenser, pre-eminently, are the voice of Renaissance England; and it would be strange if there were not a legend of wisdom among the unwritten cantos of *The Faerie Queene*. For the magnanimity of the Renaissance, as we have seen, is not only exalted 'noblesse'; it is that of the enlightened mind as well.

Looking back over the rich variety of *The Faerie Queene*, even as we have it, we are surprised to be left with a sense of inward unity and cohesion. It is not a unity derived from the structure, logical though that is in its foundation. Nor is it derived from Arthur. Although he is Magnificence, the sum of all the rest, his appearances are increasingly sporadic, less closely integrated with the adventures of each successive patron knight, and we feel that it is in the unwritten account of his own quest for Gloriana that his relationship with the whole would have been most evident. Yet the sense of unity remains.

We have looked at *The Faerie Queene*, as Spenser directed us, as a study of the individual virtues of which Magnificence is composed. It is only as the poem begins to possess his mind that the reader realizes that the name of each of the patron knights could be Love itself. The whole intricate structure is the temple of love, in which it is manifest and reverenced in all its aspects. Holiness itself is inspired and sustained by its passionate love of truth. Temperance reveals sterile lust and careless frivolity for the counterfeit of love, and sets them withering in the bright flame of reality. Chastity seeks love only where honour also is to be found; its natural fruition is marriage, as far removed from a self-regarding virginity as it is from lust, and although it delights in its own consummation it is purged of carnal taint. Love is as free as it is noble – jealousy debases the very image of humanity. In its search for the beloved it is enduring and courageous. It can deny itself for the sake of a larger duty, as Britomart leaves Arthegall free to fulfil his quest. In submission it is free, and is never so much itself as when it respects the rightful harmony of the natural order. It will not stoop to dishonourable means in hope of a return, but rather guards not only its own honour but that of all others from the breath of scandal. It is serviceable and humble wherever it finds occasion, for 'entire affection hateth nicer hands'.[1] It is indeed the very fountain of all courtesy.

Love, in fact, is the ultimate theme of Spenser's whole poem: and love is magnanimity,

> for it of honour and all vertue is
> The roote, and brings forth glorious flowres of fame
>
> (IV, Pro. 2).

But this is a far cry from Aristotle. It is not the magnanimity of classical Greece, but that of the Christian soul in quest of glory, the ultimate objective of every knight as it is of Arthur himself.

[1] I viii 40.

In that Faery Queene I meane glory in my generall intention, but in my particular I conceiue the most excellent & glorious person of our soueraine the Queene, and her kingdome in Faerye land.

Is there so great a difference as appears between Spenser's general and his particular intention? The particular intention is certainly compliment, but it is also more than compliment. Gloriana is celebrated together with her kingdom. His praise of her is also an expression of faith and pride in his own country. The country of Una and Mercilla, of Timias and Arthegall, is no mean inheritance, and Spenser's love of it breathes through every line; through the sunlit meadows and the bright waters, and the woods where the thrushes sing, as much as in the tales of heroic adventure. Here, if anywhere, men may set glory before them as an end. The splendour of that 'bright Angells towre' does not wholly outshine the splendour of Cleopolis, but rather includes it in a greater radiance. The shimmer of the heavenly towers is caught and reflected by the 'towre all built of christall cleene', across the plains of Faerie Land, as windows reflect the sun. But the greater glory is the true end of all.

Aristotle's magnanimous man was wholly self-sufficient. The medieval magnanimous man sought an honour consistent with his Christian ethic, but it was an honour chiefly to be enjoyed in the temporal world. But Spenser's magnanimous man is on a journey. His quest is to be crowned with glory in another world than this, and his magnanimity is not wholly his by nature, but by the operation of divine grace. He stands between the classical-chivalric tradition of the past and a vaster conception still – the divine magnanimity of unfallen Adam and, beyond that, of the redeeming Christ.

Chapter Six

MAGNANIMOUS TO CORRESPOND WITH HEAVEN

It is a deeply exciting experience to move from the poetry of Spenser to that of Milton. Fundamentally, both men are of the Renaissance – Spenser its high noon, and Milton its last great flame of evening light before the sun goes down. Both are themselves magnanimous spirits, men of courage and wisdom and infinite aspiration. The eyes of both are fixed upon eternity, towards which all life is pilgrimage. But there is one profound difference between them: Spenser looks forward from time to eternity, Milton looks backward from eternity to time.

Every temporal action in Milton's poetry is viewed *sub specie aeternitatis*, seen small and sharp and clear in the light that streams from God. It appears in relation to eternal action as the pendant world first appears to Satan in relation to the heaven from which it is suspended,

> in bigness as a Starr
> Of smallest Magnitude close by the Moon.

It is partly this that accounts for the remarkable unity of Milton's poetry. Other travellers on the pilgrim way see one vista succeeding to another. But Milton views the world of this life spread out beneath him as a single panorama viewed from the top of some great hill. Other poets may change their ideas as they grow in experience, so that we can distinguish clearly between their earlier and their later work. Milton's poetic idiom may change a little – the utterance grows more powerful, more varied, and finally more austere – but the intrinsic quality of his thought remains always the same. We can pick up his work at any point and find it still unchanged in essence. It is a single jewel, turned and turned against the sun, so that its facets glitter in a changing light; but the heart of fire at its centre still burns with the same steady radiance. We should expect no other of one whose sense of vocation was so high, whose vigil before taking up his sword was so long and strenuous, a discipline of soul as well as of intellect.

> He who would not be frustrate of his hope to write well hereafter in laudable things, ought himself to be a true poem; that is, a composition and pattern of the best and honourablest things; not presuming to sing high praises of heroic men, or famous cities, unless he have in himself the experience and practice of all that is praiseworthy.[1]

Milton's work has this unity chiefly because it is only the outward projection of that long poem which was his life, a poem with a single theme of magnanimity, laboured upon towards perfection.

Fundamentally his intention is the same as that of 'our sage and serious poet, Spenser', of whom he spoke with as generous and loving a tribute as any poet has ever paid to another. Perhaps it was Spenser's story of Arthur and Gloriana which chiefly deterred Milton from basing his own epic, as he had once contemplated, on

> what resounds
> In Fable or *Romance* of *Uthers* Son
> Begirt with *British* and *Armoric* Knights (I, 579–81).

Milton was to attempt an even higher theme, yet his spring of action is the same. Spenser's Arthur is to allure his readers

[1] *Apology for Smectymnuus*, 1641.

95

to 'Magnificence'. Milton's poems are to repair the neglect
of Christian commonwealths which

> teach not that to govern well is to train up a nation in true
> wisdom and virtue, and that which springs from thence
> magnanimity (take heed of that), and that which is our
> beginning, regeneration, and happiest end, likeness to God
> which in one word we call godliness.[1]

The end of poetry is one with that of learning, which is

> to repair the ruins of our first parents by regaining to know
> God aright, and out of that knowledge to love him, to imitate
> him, to be like him, as we may the nearest, by possessing our
> souls of true virtue, which, being united to the heavenly grace
> of faith, makes up the highest perfection.[2]

Virtue. Again and again the word sounds forth like a
trumpet. Reference to Bradshaw's *Concordance to the Poetical
Works of John Milton* shows that, with the single exception
of 'glory', it occurs more frequently in his poems than any
other word denoting abstract quality; and it echoes constantly throughout the prose pamphlets as well. Milton uses
it chiefly as an absolute; he wishes us to contemplate the
whole rather than analyse the parts. But when he does think
of the qualities which compose it, his anatomy of it i
remarkably like Spenser's. Michael warns Adam of a fallen
world with 'Justice and Temperance, Truth, and Faith
forgot'.[3] Adam, pondering his vision of redemption, learns

> that suffering for Truth's sake
> Is fortitude to highest victorie (XII, 569–70).

This, says Michael, is the sum of wisdom. (Again, in
'wisdom', we hear the echoes of a great word, dying away

[1] *Of Reformation in England*, 1641.   [2] *Tractate of Education*, 1644
[3] XI, 802.

backwards through time, through Spenser, and Sidney, and
far away in Chaucer.)

> onely add
> Deeds to thy knowledge answerable, add Faith,
> Add Vertue, Patience, Temperance, add Love,
> By name to come call'd Charitie, the soul
> Of all the rest (XII, 581–5).

Sir Arthegall, Sir Guyon, Red Cross and Una, Sir Calidore,
Britomart – are they not here as well? And all united, as
Spenser had united them, in the soul of love? There is little
intrinsic difference between virtue's 'goodly golden chaine'
and that golden chain on which swings the pendant world.

The knights of *The Faerie Queene* were in quest of glory, a
guerdon to be bestowed when the heavenly City was won.
Milton looks to the same end. But here is the crux of
difference: Gloriana will give herself largely of grace,
though only to one of high desert; but in Milton's universe
no such desert is possible, and glory can *only* be of grace.
The rays of Arthur's own honour will mingle with that final
light; but redeemed Adam's ultimate glory contains no
single beam of his own. He is irradiated only by the
splendour which flows from the throne of God, wholly
grace-given, the fringe of the shekinah itself. None the less,
although man can in no way earn divine grace, since there is
no good in him that is not itself given by God, he can never
be released from the duty of seeking it. The will to magnanimity is the only condition on which glory can be bestowed
This is the unchanging theme of that poem which is Milton,
though at different times it may find different utterance.

As within the movement of a symphony the theme may
first be stated simply and clearly, to be taken up and
elaborated later, so Milton's first statement is the simplest.
It is also the most Spenserian in mood.

> The first and chiefest office of love begins and ends in the soul, producing those happy twins of her divine generation, knowledge and virtue.[1]

The words might well have been an epigraph for *Comus*, the memory of which was clearly in Milton's mind when he wrote them. The Lady's virtue was not confined merely to sexual chastity and bodily temperance. It is true that she passed through the enchanted wood as Sir Guyon through Acrasia's Bower. But

> that Golden Key
> That ope's the Palace of Eternity

can be no single form of self-restraint. It can be none other than magnanimity itself, the best of which the heart is capable, the 'first and chiefest office of love'. The epilogue is a hymn of fruition, not of virginity. Just as Spenser had done, Milton sets the garden of false desire over against the garden of Adonis, where from Psyche's side

> Two blissful twins are to be born,
> Youth and Joy.

The similarity of phrasing leaves little doubt that these divinely lovely creatures are the same as 'those happy twins of her divine generation, knowledge and virtue'. *Comus* also is an anatomy of love, a poem of tremendous affirmations. It begins with heavenly love itself, in the Spirit (that diviner Ariel), who comes with such willing sacrifice to 'this dim spot, which men call earth', enduring the soil upon his 'pure ambrosial weeds'; and it ends with the promise of that same love, echoing from the starry threshold of Jove's court, that

> if Vertue feeble were,
> Heav'n itself would stoop to her.

[1] *Apology for Smectymnuus.*

98

The radiance of the Lady, crystal-bright and cold as water in moonlight, expresses love again as Britomart had done – that same passionate reverence for the whole created world, which cannot endure its abuse. And in the Elder Brother love finds the voice of fortitude and undying hope, the challenge which the Christian knight flings into the face of despair:

> Vertue may be assail'd, but never hurt,
> Surpriz'd by unjust force, but not enthrall'd,
> Yea even that which mischief meant most harm,
> Shall in the happy trial prove most glory.
> But evil on it self shall back recoyl,
> And mix no more with goodness, when at last
> Gather'd like scum, and setl'd to it self
> It shall be in eternal restless change
> Self-fed, and self-consum'd, if this fail
> The pillar'd firmament is rott'nness,
> And earths base built on stubble (ll. 589–99).

Already the great central theme of all Milton's life is stated. The 'charming cup' of love which is 'truly so' is that of virtue; and virtue is the control of passion by 'sanctitude of reason':

> Wherefore did he create passions within us, pleasures round about us, but that these rightly tempered are the very ingredients of virtue?

> When God gave him [Adam] reason, He gave him freedom to choose, for reason is but choosing.

So Milton had argued in the *Areopagitica*, so God the Father affirms in *Paradise Lost* – 'reason also is choice'.

In *Paradise Lost* the original theme of the symphony is repeated, enriched, and elaborated. Reason is choice: but choice confronts the protagonists in different ways which, by their contrasts and relationships, sustain the dramatic tension of the whole epic. The right choice, the magnanimous choice, is absolute in the Son, conditional in the angels, precariously balanced in Adam, and rejected in Satan. All of them, whether by action or negation, make clear to us what is Miltonic magnanimity.

At once we are aware of an emphasis not found in Spenser. Whether in angels or men, magnanimity is dependent on a prerequisite: it can be found only within a creaturely relationship with God. It is only by his relation to his Creator that Adam is capable of virtue at all. In him shines truth, wisdom, and sanctitude, but only 'in true filial freedom plac'd'. His original majesty derives from obedience itself. He is made of express purpose that he

> endu'd
> With Sanctitude of Reason, might erect
> His Stature, and upright with Front serene
> Govern the rest, self-knowing, and from thence
> Magnanimous to correspond with Heav'n,
> But grateful to acknowledge whence his good
> Descends (VII, 507–13).

His magnanimity in a state of innocence repeats that of the angels themselves, with whom he shares in adoration, freely and delightedly given – the divine paradox of freedom which makes obedience its choice. It is only Satan who, grudging to acknowledge himself a creature, becomes even in heaven a slave who 'servilly ador'd Heav'ns awful Monarch'. The rest, rejoicing in their creaturely estate, are free.

> My self and all th'Angelic Host that stand
> In sight of God enthron'd, our happie state
> Holds, as you yours, while our obedience holds;

> On other surety none; freely we serve
> Because we freely love, as in our will
> To love or not; in this we stand or fall (V, 535-40).

By this Adam himself is in honour the equal of the angels:

> Nor less think wee in Heav'n of thee on Earth
> Then of our fellow servant, and inquire
> Gladly into the wayes of God with Man:
> For God we see hath honour'd thee, and set
> On Man his equal Love (VIII, 224-8).

Here is the ground of virtue, the only condition which makes love possible. While it is based upon obedience, Adam and Eve enjoy so full and glorious a mutual love that it moves Satan himself first to awe and admiration and then to an anguish of envy. Such love is itself a form of rational choice which, through the human affections, should mount at last to the divine:

> In loving thou dost well, in passion not,
> Wherein true Love consists not; love refines
> The thoughts, and heart enlarges, hath his seat
> In Reason, and is judicious, is the scale
> By which to heav'nly Love thou maist ascend (VIII, 588-92).

In this Platonic conception Milton is not rejecting the love of the heart or senses. No other writer has evoked such a picture of innocent sensuousness as Adam and Eve's in their unfallen splendour, nor contemplated the pleasures of the body with such reverent delight. But at the very first moment when such pleasure is snatched at as a thing of right, and not accepted as a gift of God, love itself is destroyed, both human and divine. The real heartbreak of *Paradise Lost* is less the moment of the Fall than the distortion of love's glory to a thing of shame. Who can endure the moment when Adam and Eve, skulking in the garden, are called forth to face the judgement and the mercy of the Son?

> Love was not in thir looks, either to God
> Or to each other, but apparent guilt,
> And shame, and perturbation, and despaire (X, 111–13).

None can depict more potently and terrifyingly than Milton the anguish for lost innocence. Robbed of his creaturely obedience, man is robbed also of love and adoration and delight. Without it his whole vision of life is distorted. The God who had smiled upon him face to face in the Garden, the angels who had been his guardians and guests and fellow servants, these have become 'Our great Forbidder and his Spies'. What other purpose can there be for fallen man, so self-deceiving, than that which Milton has proposed, to open his long-blinded eyes and to 'regain to know God aright'?

Yet Milton is writing epic, not tragedy, and his hero is distinctively conceived as an epic hero, whose function it is to exhibit greatness, to inspire the reader to the emulation of nobility. The near-infinite capacity of man is his theme as much as the *felix culpa* of the Fall itself. The non-Paradisal world which Adam and Eve inherit is not a second-best, for all the vast pattern of human anguish which Michael foreshows them. They lose that nostalgic world of childhood, which memory presents to every generation as the garden where the sun always shone; a world which we always long for at our best moments when we look at the smirched pattern of our adult life, but a world to which none of us would really return if given the choice. The range of the knowledge of good and evil is so great that we feel it worth all cost, and are prepared to buy growth into full experience at the price of Paradise. So Adam, as the memory and promise of perfect magnanimity, is never dwarfed by the vast stage upon which he moves. His entrance is so prepared that all preceding episodes throw their beams full upon him; the glow of Hell's dark fires, the pure ethereal stream of heavenly light, the serene clarity of Eden, all converge upon Adam and Eve. Man is the first word of the poem, his existence and his future the theme of discourse both in Heaven and Hell, yet we are made to wait for his appearance while expectation rises; and when at last we see him, the first word is of majesty. Except God Himself, there is no limit to his lordliness. 'Led on, yet sinless, with desire to know' (the insatiable thirst of the Renaissance), he is instructed by angels, and his knowledge is commensurate with theirs, though his is 'discursive', theirs 'intuitive'. There is no ignorance in Paradise; Milton is quite specific that neither Adam nor Eve is seeking true intellectual wisdom from their disobedience. The wisdom of that first unspotted magnanimity ('the cleernesse hool of sapience' as Chaucer called it) lay in the condition of Adam's greatest dignity, his obedience, which endowed him with power to give to God Himself, being otherwise unable to 'perform aught whereof hee hath need'. This is that Adam of forgotten memory, magnanimous by birthright rather than discipline, whom his corrupted children can see only in vision and that imperfectly.

If Adam in innocence shows human magnanimity as it should be – a correspondency with heaven in obedience, adoration, and love – Satan by negation shows it almost as clearly. For Satan has a spurious magnanimity of his own, still more misleading to the unwary because it yet has traces in it of the true magnanimity which he must once have had in heaven. He has the courage which should belong to it, but a courage which, grounded in insolence and despair, degenerates into foolhardiness, the rashness condemned by Aristotle. He has the spring of compassion still rising within him, but the waters are bitter; whether it is for the fallen angels or doomed Adam, it issues in remorse, but not in repentance. Where he professes pity he brings destruction, pleading necessity as his excuse – a word used by Satan only. But reason is choice; and Satan stands self-condemned, as self-deceived, in so disguising his wilful persistence in evil, for Milton will admit no necessity above that of the will dedicated to God. Virtue itself has still some hold upon him, enough to make him homesick for its beauty when he meets it in the challenge of the youthful Zephon, yet it issues only in frustration and personal vanity:

> abasht the Devil stood,
> And felt how awful goodness is, and saw
> Vertue in her shape how lovly, saw, and pin'd
> His loss; but chiefly to find here observ'd
> His lustre visibly impar'd (IV, 846–50).

Significantly, Satan resembles Aristotle's magnanimous man in the one respect which the Christian tradition has so greatly modified. He is self-pride incarnate. St Paul would have said, wisely, that he spoke as a fool. In the pagan world, the man who founded his pride on his own worth was following the highest that he could attain. He might become arrogant, but he was not likely to be dishonourable. But he who, in a world (whether natural or supernatural) which recognizes God as creator and benefactor, relies solely upon himself, is building on a false foundation. He has rejected the perfect for the imperfect, the original for that which is derived from it. Reason is choice: and he who deliberately prefers the lesser to the greater falls at once into falsehood and evil. It is the survival in Milton's Satan of the purely classical sentiment of 'proper pride' which marks him as a travesty of the magnanimous man in the full Renaissance use of the word. Such glimmerings of virtue as remain in him serve only to add a distorted malignancy to evil. And as even these sparks grow fainter, he grows less and less the fallen Lucifer, son of the morning, and more and more the Devil who is very near the brute. His disguisings are increasingly debased, from spurious cherub to the squatting toad, the creeping mist, the serpent shorn of its glory and its traditional wisdom and become mere brute. As we turn the jewel of Milton's poetry against the sun it catches once again a familiar light, reflecting back to *Comus*:

> So dear to Heav'n is Saintly chastity,
> That when a soul is found sincerely so,
> A thousand liveried Angels lacky her,
> Driving far off each thing of sin and guilt,
> And in cleer dream, and solemn vision
> Tell her of things that no gross ear can hear,
> Till oft convers with heav'nly habitants
> Begin to cast a beam on th'outward shape,
> The unpolluted temple of the mind,
> And turns it by degrees to the souls essence,
> Till all be made immortal: but when lust
> By unchaste looks, loose gestures, and foul talk,
> But most by leud and lavish act of sin,
> Lets in defilement to the outward parts,
> The soul grows clotted by contagion,
> Imbodies and imbrutes, till she quite loose
> The divine property of her first being (ll. 453–69).

Where unfallen Adam is truly magnanimous, Satan is a magnificent sham, and image after image reminds us of it. He lives in a hollow world, the paradoxical horror of a shapeless and shifting infinity within an imprisoning vault. The claustrophobic nightmare of hell is intensified by the mocking suggestion of endless space; but always there is the enclosing shell, from which the echoes rebound with thinner and thinner clamour.

> He call'd so loud, that all the hollow Deep
> Of Hell resounded.

Again and again we are reminded of his 'semblance of worth, not substance', and this inner emptiness is projected into hell itself, where the thunder bellows as if confined in some great dome; where Belial's 'false and hollow' tongue counsels an empty hope and Mammon's lunatic rhetoric fetches applause

> as when hollow Rocks retain
> The sound of blustring winds.

Only the most careless of readers could mistake Satan's 'unconquerable will' for true magnanimous courage.

Only in the Son is magnanimity absolute, but in him it is a virtue beyond mortal striving. Readers who are troubled by the legalistic arguments of the Father sometimes forget that, however unorthodox Milton's theology may still be thought to be, he mirrors the Father completely in the Son. If love and compassion abound in the Son it is only because they first abound in the Father:

> in him all his Father shon
> Substantially express'd, and in his face
> Divine compassion visibly appeerd,
> Love without end, and without measure Grace (III, 139-42).

But this, even for Milton's eagle sight, is in a world dark with excess of light, beyond the reach of human aspiration.

Yet divine magnanimity is indeed the ideal which Milton would have men to follow. And so the theme is introduced again, in yet another form.

Adam's magnanimity was not strong enough to save him from the Fall. It is a virtue derived from heaven itself, and only in one divine can it be perfectly displayed. Yet, if men are not to fall into the despair of Satan, which merely envies the virtue it cannot reach, they must see it displayed in one who is also a man. For this reason Milton especially stresses the humanity of the incarnate Christ, 'This perfect Man, by merit call'd my son'.

In comparison with the other works which we have studied, both of Milton and his predecessors, there is an extraordinary stillness at the heart of *Paradise Regained*. Adventure and action have hitherto been the very body of the ideal, and Christ also has in him the capacity for noble endeavour and 'amplitude of mind to greatest Deeds'. Yet it is in endurance rather than in action that we see his magnanimity explicit. The temptation of the first Adam is reenacted in the wilderness and, like his, it demands steadfastness to withstand rather than courage to do. Satan's actual defeat is here. The Crucifixion itself is no more than the outward event inevitably deriving from it, just as the advent of Death into the world was the outward event inevitably deriving from the Fall. It is the consequence of choice and not the moment of choice itself. But, for all his stillness, there is nothing passive in the Christ of *Paradise Regained*. He has tremendous dignity and power. He is as rightly conscious of his own merit as is Aristotle's magnanimous man, but for different reasons. Indeed, he specifically rejects the philosophy of the Stoic, and surely has Aristotle also in mind when speaking so sternly of

> his vertuous man,
> Wise, perfect in himself, and all possessing
> Equal to God (IV, 301–3).

Christ's sense of worth is not founded on such self-sufficiency but, like unfallen Adam's, on his relationship with God. He, God's son, moves with absolute authority in God's world; but it is an authority grounded in obedience. In him are all the qualities of magnanimity – courage, steadfastness, compassion, high-heartedness. But beyond all this, transforming it with an eternal light, is the magnanimity of God Himself, the divine sacrifice by which

> to give a kingdom hath been thought
> Greater and nobler done, and to lay down
> Far more magnanimous, then to assume (II, 481–3).

The other heroes of the tradition have all excelled in action; this is a destined victim. But here is no passive sacrifice; the giving and the laying down are the most deliberate action. This is that central point of existence, the 'still centre of the turning world', where movement appears stillness, and where suffering is the most perfect form of action.

Christ is not only the Redeemer; he is the type also of 'the true wayfaring Christian',[1] whose end indeed is glory. But this is not a heavenly apotheosis of earthly glory. It is of a wholly different kind, for

> why should man seek glory? who of his own
> Hath nothing (IV, 301–2).

[1] This more usual reading, 'wayfaring', expresses an image so familiar in traditional Christian thought that Milton may well have used it in the original *Areopagitica*; although in three extant copies, which probably passed through his own hands, it has been emended to 'warfaring'. See *The Works of John Milton*, Columbia University Press, 1931, Vol. IV, note to pp. 366–7.

There is only one true glory in the universe, that of the shekinah itself; but by the grace of God man may at last rest within its light. Even for Messiah himself it has not yet fully come, and the poem ends in the profoundest stillness:

> Hee unobserv'd
> Home to his Mothers house private return'd.

Milton has shown us in *Comus* the pattern of virtue. In *Paradise Lost* he has shown us what it must once have been in the original majesty of innocence. In *Paradise Regained* he has shown it divinely manifested in a human form. But both Adam and Christ are unique. What magnanimity may be achieved by man as he now is?

In *Samson Agonistes* the ageing Milton presents an epilogue to the long poem which was his life. In Samson, the projection of himself, he struggles with the problem of how fallen man can avail himself of redemption and regain his forfeited virtue. It is a central paradox of the Christian faith that man cannot deserve grace by any effort of his own, and yet without effort he cannot attain to it. No quest for personal honour will lead him to his end. How then is the way to be found? In *Samson Agonistes* Milton finds the answer.

Samson cannot begin where innocent Adam did, but he is still of heroic mould, and great chiefly in his acknowledgement of the heavenly power within him,

> great in hopes
> With youthful courage and magnanimous thoughts
> Of birth from Heav'n foretold (ll. 523–5).

His self-betrayal runs the same course as Adam's, prompted like his by pride and unbridled passion, and ends in the same lassitude of near-despair.

Nature within me seems
In all her functions weary of herself;
My race of glory done, and race of shame (ll. 595–7).

He is haunted by the 'sense of Heav'ns desertion'. But then, slowly and painfully, he relearns his lost obedience, finding in it at last a deeper and richer meaning than before. His father's lamentations lead him to admit the depth of his own fault, and he is content to be forgotten, in a spirit of utter dependence admitting that

All the contest is now
'Twixt God and *Dagon* (ll. 461–2).

The visit of Dalila – 'weakness then with weakness come to parl' – with her assumption of their common corruption is, with its grain of truth, a part of his purgative suffering. But in repudiating the false beauty which could still allure him 'with secret sting of amorous remorse' he wins back part of himself. The insults of Harapha then wake in him a salutary rage. The Philistine giant voices Samson's own inward fears of God's desertion and, compelling him thus to answer them, unwittingly recalls him from his previous despair, and reminds him of returning strength. And at last, summoned for the second time to the feast of Dagon, he is prophetically aware that some last act of obedience is now demanded from him. He goes out to an unknown future, with will wholly yielded, to find his own redemption in the deliverance of Israel. It is not only the demand of the Greek tragic form which causes Samson's death to be recounted rather than seen. For again the victory was already won in the period of steadfast endurance, and the outward act was but the epilogue. Suffering has once more transcended action.

The poem ends in a shout of triumph, followed by one of those moments of profound and satisfied peace in which so many of the great Miltonic harmonies have their close. Once again Milton has vindicated the ways of God to men; and once again he has shown that they are not only the ways of mercy, but of grace abounding. For Samson has regained more than his first obedience. Out of the evil of his sin, as out of Adam's, has come a greater good. He has lost an ignorant and easy goodness, a virtue unexercised and unbreathed; but through harsh experience and bitter effort he has learned a new relationship with God, an absolute trust in the darkness as well as in the light, and can offer up a will hardened and tempered by endurance.

There is no way back to the Paradise of innocence. The gate is shut and the bright sword guards it, and the face of innocence itself has become alien and terrible as Adam and Eve look back at the threatening walls. But the golden chain still holds between earth and heaven, and there is another way to be found. The magnanimity of the Christian may yet lead back to the Tree of Life which grows by the Tree of Knowledge, and through experience and sorrow he enters into a new and profounder relationship with his God. Nor does he walk that way alone:

> which is best and happiest yet, all this
> With God not parted from him, as was feard,
> But favouring and assisting to the end (ll. 1718–20).

Once again the jewel catches a familiar light from the 'starry threshold' of an earlier vision –

> if vertue feeble were,
> Heaven itself would stoop to her.

The quest of magnanimity begins in the grace of God, and ends in the shadow of his glory.

Chapter Seven

LIGHT OF COMMON DAY

The Magnanimous Man has been traced from Aristotle to Milton, through tales of chivalry, pastoral, and heroic poetry. Through four centuries of English life we can see in him the ideal of many living men, from the young de Joinville (a comparatively small man among so many of the greater nobility) who left his quiet French estates to follow St Louis to Palestine, to Fulke Greville, Sidney's friend and biographer. That many lesser men admired the same picture can be seen from the spate of 'courtesy books' which appeared in constant succession from early Tudor times to the late sixteenth century: Sir Thomas Elyot's *The Governour* (1531), the anonymous *Institucion of a Gentleman* (1555), Castiglione's *The Courtier* ('done into Englyshe by Thomas Hoby' in 1561), Joseph Hall's *Characters of Virtues and Vices* (1608), Francis Markham's *Book of Honour* (1625), William Higford's *Institutions, or Advice to his Grandson* (1658), and many others, written for the instruction and inspiration of young people of good family, are all concerned with the true ground of honour and magnanimity. But it is worth noting that the earliest of these books were written by courtiers and men of fashion, while the later ones come from the smaller gentry. Higford, for instance, was the squire of a small and charming Gloucestershire manor,[1] still remote even today; and he recalls with the wistful pride of one who has seen greater days how he once saw

> Sir James Scudamore, your thrice noble Grandfather, enter the Tiltyard in a handsome equipage, all in compleate Armor,

[1] Dixton Manor, Alderton.

embelished with Plumes, his Beaver close, mounted upon a very high bounding horse (I have seen the shooes of his horse glitter above the heads of all the people) and when he came to the encounter or shock, brake as many Spears as the most, her Majesty Q Elizabeth, with a Train of Ladies, like the Starrs in the Firmament, and the whole Court looking upon him with a very gratious aspect.[1]

No more such tournaments, no more such playing at knights in Commonwealth England. The cult of magnanimity itself is passing from the great to the lesser gentry, like an outmoded fashion.

By Higford's day one suspects that it was indeed becoming outmoded, even though *Paradise Lost, Paradise Regained,* and *Samson Agonistes* are yet to come. For Milton's is the solitary voice of one fallen on evil days and evil times; he is the last enormous wave of a receding tide. And, by a curious paradox, there is a change in the concept of magnanimity, secretly operative in his own poetry, which is one of the causes leading ultimately to the Magnanimous Man's disappearance as a literary hero. For centuries it had developed from a classical-humanist way of thought, a confidence in man's potential greatness, which could be expressed in terms of achievement. In Sidney and Spenser this confidence can still be harmonized with Christian thought, while leaving the initiative of goodness, as it were, with the Christian knight himself. But Milton, who sees virtue wholly in terms of obedience, of the devoted will, of steadfast adherence to an act of choice, has narrowed the field of action and achievement to a single point. Magnanimity has hitherto been a virtue to be exercised by man in relation to other men; its possessor strives for the common good. Milton himself was possessed of it, and none was more

[1] Op. cit., p. 69.

conscious than he of public duty. But in his poetry he shows his hero in an increasingly isolated relationship with God. The fate of others depends indeed upon his choice, but the choice is made only with reference to God's demand upon the individual soul. Imperceptibly, magnanimity is becoming an ideal of the heart on its own secret course rather than of the social group, and is displayed as often in patient suffering as in positive action.

Nor is Milton alone in this. The emphasis on the secret conscience, the soul alone with its God, is in tune with the quietist personal piety of the Anglican divines of the seventeenth century. Traherne defines magnanimity with a passion of delighted reverence, an exaltation as great as that of any of the poets who had celebrated it before him. But it is the exaltation of the mystic, the visionary, listening to 'things that no gross ear can hear':

> Magnanimity and Contentment are very near allyed, like Brothers and Sisters they spring from the same Parents, but are of several Features. Fortitude and Patience are Kindred too to this incomparable Vertue. . . . It includes all that belongs to a *Great Soul*: A high and mighty Courage, an invincible Patience, an immoveable Grandeur which is above the reach of Injuries, a contempt of all little and feeble Enjoyments, and a certain kind of Majesty that is conversant only with Great things; a high and lofty frame of Spirit, allayed with the sweetness of Courtesie and Respect; a deep and stable Resolution founded on Humility without any baseness; an infinite Hope; and a vast Desire; a Divine, profound, uncontrolable sense of ones own Capacity, a generous Confidence, and a great inclination to Heroical deeds; all these conspire to compleat it, with a severe and mighty expectation of Bliss incomprehensible. It soars up to Heaven, and looks down upon all the dominion of Fortune with pity and disdain. Its aims and designs are transcendent to all the Concerns of this little World.

Its Objects and its Ends are worthy of a Soul that is like GOD in Nature; and nothing less than the Kingdom of GOD, his Life and Image; nothing beneath the Friendship and Communion with him, can be its satisfaction. The Terrours, Allurements, and Censures of Men are the dust of its feet: their Avarice and Ambition are but feebleness before it. Their riches and Contentions, and Interests and Honours, but insignificant and empty trifles. All the World is but a little Bubble, Infinity and Eternity the only great and soveraign things wherewith it converseth. A Magnanimous Soul is alwaies awake. The whole globe of the Earth is but a Nutshell in comparison of its enjoyments. The Sun is its Lamp, the Sea its Fishpond, the Stars its Jewels, Men, Angels its Attendance, and GOD alone its soveraign Delight and supream Complacency. The Earth is its Garden, all Palaces its Summer houses, Cities are its Cottages, Empires its more spacious Courts, all Ages and Kingdoms its Demeans, Monarchs its Ministers and publick Agents, the whole Catholick Church its Family, the eternal Son of GOD its Pattern and Example. Nothing is great if compared to a *Magnanimous Soul*, but the Soveraign Lord of all Worlds. . . . This is the Offspring of the *Will*, the true and genuine Vertue. . . . In the poor it is more marvellous than in the Great and Rich. . . . Though their attempt appear a ridiculous madness to them to whom the Verities of Religion appear incredible, yet they are no whit discouraged or disheartened at the matter, but stoutly march on, being animated by the alarum of such a Trumpet, such a Drum as Magnanimity is.[1]

Much of this echoes Spenser and his predecessors. But, although the end of the Faerie quest was glory, the 'concerns of this little world' were its necessary field of action, whereas Traherne's has become a highly personal religious ideal. It can no longer be celebrated, as it was in *The Faerie Queene*, in a work embodying the common vision of a whole

[1] Thomas Traherne, *Christian Ethicks*, Chap. XXVIII (1675).

society. This is a change in values inevitable in a period in which personal piety begins to supersede a more corporate religious consciousness, when contemplation tends to withdraw the worshipper's attention from the world of temporal action. The concept is thus weakened from within by a simultaneous intensification yet narrowing of spiritual vision.

At the same time, and much more forcibly, it is suffering attack from without – an attack which attained its full force during Milton's life-time, but which had begun much earlier, from the time when drama became the predominant literary expression of Elizabethan England. The Magnanimous Man can live happily in the world of epic or heroic-romantic narrative because everything in it is on his own scale: but Elizabethan drama, on the other hand, breathes the air of common life; its heroes may have many of the qualities of magnanimity, but the ideal type, 'whole, perfect in himself', cannot be translated to it without loss. He is essentially non-dramatic, and being so is ultimately rejected by the theatre.

Epic and English Renaissance drama have different ends in view. The epic hero shows the potentiality of man at his greatest – not what we achieve, but what we should like to achieve. He is a star to steer by, a perfect inspiration to an imperfect world. The dramatic hero, however, holds his audience by showing us what we are or may actually become for good or ill. He may be engaged in actions as improbable as Prospero's, but the springs of action are human motives and passions as we know them in ordinary life. The very essence of such drama is the conflict of motive, whereas the magnanimous man has passed beyond conflict into the serenity of the dedicated will. Not for him the stresses of ambition or desire, the agonizing conscience, the horrors of death. He can face 'wrong, oppression, and the axe's edge' with the same unshaken confidence. Wholeness is his very nature, just as warring elements are the very nature of the dramatic hero.

Once, and once only, does an Elizabethan dramatist attempt a hero so great as to be almost beyond the reach of ordinary human conflict. He succeeds by a miracle of poetry, but a second could not have done so, and Marlowe attempted no other Tamburlaine. This Scythian shepherd sweeps from conquest to conquest, meeting as little resistance, either in the outer world or within his own heart, as the forest offers to the fire. There may be an occasional moment of self-questioning. Some thought may wander in his restless head of a grace beyond understanding, but he never allows it to tease him for more than a moment. Through scene after scene 'holding the Fates bound fast in iron chains', he owed his popular success largely to those two qualities of magnanimity which were most evident to the popular imagination – magnificence and courage. He belongs to an age which was itself magnificent, delighting in lavish profusion and display. It is not only the Countess of Shrewsbury who immortalizes her ambition and her arrogance in the stone of Hardwick Hall. The politic Cecil plans Theobalds for his old age and his son rebuilds Hatfield. The costly silks and velvets of the courtiers, the great diamond set in emeralds on a rope of 600 fair white pearls, which Leicester leaves to Elizabeth, the fortune which Raleigh spends on jewels for his shoe, are matched at a different level by the golden plates and goblets and the furred gowns of London's merchants. The pageants and the progresses, the City banquets, the splendour of the Royal Exchange itself, all speak of a world which the sheer lavishness of *Tamburlaine* will rouse to admiration. Tamburlaine's entertainment of his prisoners 'might in noble minds be counted princely'. The bold symbolism of his changing colours, the white, the scarlet, and the black, as he besieges Damascus, derives from medieval romance, but appeals also to the contemporary love of ostentation. The glitter of his sunbright armour, the splendour of imagery, dazzle the mind with their wealth:

> A hundred Tartars shall attend on thee,
> Mounted on steeds swifter than Pegasus;
> Thy garments shall be made of Median silk,
> Enchased with precious jewels of mine own,
> More rich and valurous than Zenocrate's.
> With milk-white harts upon an ivory sled,
> Thou shalt be drawn amidst the frozen pools,
> And scale the icy mountains' lofty tops,
> Which with thy beauty will be soon resolved
>
> (Part I, I ii 93–101).

Magnificence on such a scale is more than material; it touches and liberates the imagination until 'the sweet fruition of an earthly crown' becomes a symbol of spiritual aspiration rather than the satisfaction of personal ambition.

But Tamburlaine is not the Magnanimous Man. His courage rivals his magnificence and, like it, although expressed in physical terms outsoars material limit: but it differs wholly in quality from the courage of Launcelot or Red Cross. It is the courage of the medieval Alexander, violent, impetuous, and ultimately self-regarding. When the word 'magnanimity' occurs it is limited to an Alexandrian or Aristotelian sense. Tamburlaine rewards his followers with titles deserved 'by valour and by magnanimity', clearly restricting his meaning to personal courage. Dying, he exhorts his son to show a Stoic endurance of the inevitable:

> Nor bar thy mind that magnanimity
> That nobly must admit necessity (Part II, V iii 100–1).

The tragedy of Tamburlaine derives indeed from this particular limitation of his magnanimity rather than from conflict due to any other cause. His nature is human, his aspiration godlike. There is no god beyond himself whom he acknowledges, no divine source of trust or power, nothing to save this human god when time destroys mortality. No age was more aware than his of the tragic paradox of man's aspiration and his transience, and the Elizabethan audience well knew that from triumph to triumph the conqueror marched upon his own extinction. Beneath the rhodomontade and the trumpets sounds like a muffled drum-beat the approach of his last end. With the death of his loved Zenocrate his world splits apart as with an earthquake crack, in the moment of insane defiance which would try to check death itself by the physical force to which he has always trusted:

> Casane and Theridamas, to arms!

The violent irrelevance of it shocks us like some natural cataclysm. The rest of the play is but a swift decline to total ruin, when Aristotelian courage and self-sufficiency and endurance face mere annihilation, and there is nothing beyond:

> Shall sickness prove me now to be a man
> That have been termed the terror of the world?
>
> (Part II, V iii 44-5).

This is no Prince Arthur; but he is sufficiently far removed from the inward conflicts and limitations of most ordinary men to show how uneasily the irresistible hero fits into a dramatic setting. For Tamburlaine balances on the knife-edge between the sublime and the absurd, and the precarious nature of his greatness is apparent in the occasional irreverent echo of his words which we hear from some of his contemporaries in spite of their admiration.

119

So it is that, although magnanimity itself is not rejected, it is displayed only imperfectly. For the dramatic hero, as for the ordinary man, it is an aspiration towards an ideal only sometimes achieved. Some measure of failure makes him credible, although his failures are more often an Aristotelian excess than a defect of the virtue. Coriolanus has the necessary courage and greatness of spirit, but is so resentful of affront that, through his own seeking, he finds his mercy and his honour at difference within him. Antony has the grace and generosity which Coriolanus lacks; but his inevitable fall is brought about by the two weaknesses of unbridled passion and rashness, which the completely magnanimous man would have controlled. Yet it is this which convinces us of his greatness, for a lesser man could not have failed in these particulars. Only a man of high and generous heart could so love and dare beyond the bounds of reason: the cautious Augustus can control his quite genuine affection in order to make a political expedient of his sister's marriage, can so exercise judgement that he sinks into intrigue. Both in speech and action Antony has that touch of magnificent exaggeration which gives the play its spaciousness, its physical and imaginative correspondence with the magnanimity of the hero by which both, recipro-cally, are increased. He needs room in which to move and he has the world to move in. He gives a kingdom 'for a mirth'; and the cold voice of Caesar, who could give nothing himself, only serves to emphasize the extravagant generosity of the gesture. He leaves a world in ruins; but Shakespeare knew, as Spenser did, that the destruction was caused not by the vices apparently opposed to magnanimity but by the distortion of its virtues. Passion and rashness are the 'extremes' of love and courage, the extravagance of greatness.

Perhaps in *Julius Caesar* there was one conscious attempt to reconcile dramatic probability with the ideal. Brutus is the very pattern of Aristotelian *megalopsychia*. He has the general good at heart, but he lives chiefly for the name of honour:

> What is it that you would impart to me?
> If it be aught toward the general good,
> Set honour in one eye, and death i' the other,
> And I will look on both indifferently:
> For let the gods so speed me, as I love
> The name of honour more than I fear death (I ii 84–89).

The initial torment of his indecision, wherein his mind suffers the nature of an insurrection, may seem out of character in a Stoic philosopher, although dramatically essential if he is to retain the sympathy of the audience; but through the mounting tension and the final terror of the assassination scene he alone retains his confidence and his absolute self-command. He endures physical hardship and the shock of grief with the same unchanging fortitude. He takes his last farewell of Cassius with Stoic fatalism. Here, if anywhere, is Aristotelian magnanimity. Nature may stand up and say to all the world, 'This was a man'. And yet, in the final test of the audience's sympathy, Brutus too often fails.

Nothing shows more clearly than this how much warmth and vitality the magnanimous ideal has derived from a Christian context. For here, in a classical setting, it strikes unexpectedly cold. One can feel admiration, and even moments of intense sympathy; but too often Brutus' conscious rectitude verges on self-satisfaction rather than self-respect, and chills our response to him. It may be admirable Stoicism which leads him, within a minute of

Caesar's death, to argue that in killing his friend he had done
him service:

> So are we Caesar's friends, that have abridg'd
> His time of fearing death (III i 105–6).

But, measured by this, Mark Antony's double-dealing seems
frank and ingenuous. It may be unswerving integrity which
prompts Brutus to condemn his friend's conduct, but one
cannot help echoing Cassius' retort:

> A friendly eye would never see such faults.

The first repression of grief for Portia's death is sincerely
moving; but when for the second time the news is pressed
upon him he is rather too self-consciously concerned to play
the philosopher in public:

> Why farewell, Portia. We must die, Messala:
> With meditating that she must die once,
> I have the patience to endure it now (IV iii 190–2).

Shakespeare himself seems aware of some failure in sympathy, for he goes to unusual pains to reflect his hero's
virtues in the admiration of his fellows. But he is never
wholly successful. In Brutus is displayed the one innate
weakness of the pagan magnanimous man. Self-reliance is
dangerously close to self-satisfaction.

The ideal is seen more happily, but also more confusedly,
in Shakespeare's Henry V. The 'legerity of courage', the
clemency, the liberality of the magnanimous man are all
displayed at times in 'this star of England' with his

> largess universal like the sun. . . .
> Thawing cold fear (IV, Prol.).

But he is still far removed from the absolute figure of epic,
not conceived in those great and simple terms only, but in

the subtler complexities of ordinary life; and we are engrossed, also, as much by the political immediacy of the theme as by personal moral issues.

It seems then that in the realistic theatre the ideal cannot be successfully portrayed without some modification. Yet it is so deeply ingrained in the moral tradition and, for the generation of Sidney and Spenser, so present to the literary consciousness, that it can hardly be ignored. There are only two possible ways for the dramatist to absorb it, and both will be equally destructive. One is to move further away from realism, from drama to melodrama. The other is to satirize it.

An ideal type almost inevitably generates a satirical antitype, saving us from pomposity by a natural sense of proportion; and it may seem odd that this should not have occurred earlier in relation to magnanimity. Chaucer indeed, secure in the ideal, could afford to laugh at it a little. There is a delicate hint of absurdity in *The Knight's Tale*, in the young Squire himself, and even perhaps in the extension of 'noblesse' to the 'Briton clerk' in *The Franklin's Tale*. Perhaps also the exquisite Sir Topas, with his dauntless vow that

> the geaunt shal be deed,
> Bityde what bityde!

glances sidelong at chivalry as well as at 'rym dogerel'. Yet there is no specific satire. As long as the age of chivalry lasted, the gap between ideal and reality was not sufficiently apparent to invite laughter. But the social changes of the later sixteenth century produced a very different situation. Knights had ceased to be a military force for something more than a century; yet an annual 'tournament' was still held to celebrate the accession of Queen Elizabeth, for which courtiers went to fantastic expense in vying with one another in the magnificence of their dress and armour. A chivalric code was being preserved as something of a fashionable cult. And no longer was the court confined to the older aristocracy, whose grandfathers at least had been bred to the knightly code. 'The Lords and Gentlemen that ran' in the tournament before the Queen on 17 November 1590, included men such as Henry Nowell and Thomas Gerrard, whose families had risen through the practice of law, as the Cecils themselves had done; William Gresham, descended from city mercers and financiers of genius; Lord Compton, who married the daughter of Sir John Spencer, Lord Mayor of London from 1594-5, who had made a vast fortune in the Mediterranean and Levant trade. Even Sir Henry Lee, Master of the Armory, who retired from his office at this same tournament, owed his wealth to his great flocks of sheep (although Aubrey repeats a story that he 'was supposed brother of Queen Elizabeth'). These men, even when they played at chivalry, may well have felt the cult to be at least a little bogus. In the same way the writer's audience has been extended, and the citizen as well as the courtier can read poetry and attend plays – a situation very soon to be evident in drama itself. Sooner or later an established tradition of thought or conduct will lose its impetus and give way to change. There is no need to look far for external causes; it will in any case exhaust itself from within. It is then, while the old habit of thought still finds expression, but the spirit within begins to fail, that the young and brilliant writer discovers his opportunity. Shakespeare seized his in the most immediately topical of all his comedies, *Love's Labour's Lost*. While the celebration of magnanimity is still finding its greatest advocates in Sidney and Spenser, and Milton is yet to come, the satirical anti-type has already arrived.

On the courtly level, full of charm and wit and elegantly fashionable poetry, *Love's Labour's Lost* tells the story of the King of Navarre and his three courtiers who, having vowed to forswear women's company for a twelvemonth of study, fall immediately in love with the Princess of France and her ladies and – being thus forsworn – are each assigned a year's penance before they can attain their loves. It is prettily contrived, and must have greatly pleased the ear of the young men of fashion. But the barb of the play is the 'magnificent Armado', the Spanish don whose love for the country wench, Jaquenetta (who is no better than she should be), parodies that of the courtiers for their mistresses.

Armado is a delight in himself, but it is fairly certain that he caricatures not only a type but an individual. It is impossible for a later generation to pick up all the threads of a play as topical as this, but one cannot doubt that Armado, with his accent, his extravagant dress, his love, and his literary pretensions, suggested a skit upon Sir Walter Raleigh.[1] He is, of course, a great deal more than this, but the topical references cannot be ignored. If the first version of *Love's Labour's Lost* belongs to 1593, Raleigh was already identified with the literary cult of magnanimity. He had been the recipient of the prefatory letter to *The Faerie Queene*, published with the first three books, in which we are told that Prince Arthur represents Magnificence. Spenser is careful at no time to suggest any identification of Raleigh with Prince Arthur. Instead, he figures him clearly enough in Arthur's squire, Timias, whose misfortunes in Book III seem to reflect Raleigh's temporary loss of the Queen's favour in 1589. Timias is of humble birth; Belphoebe in

---

[1] For a full discussion of this possible identification see M. C. Bradbrook, *The School of Night*, 1936; F. A. Yates, *A Study of 'Love's Labour's Lost'*, 1936; and W. Oakeshott, *The Queen and the Poet*, 1960.

curing him of his physical wound inflicts a greater wound
upon his heart, to be healed only by one 'sovereign salve'
which she denies him. He dare not confess his love, for

> When his mean estate he did review
> He from such hardy boldness was restrained (III v 44).

Everything builds up a picture of passionate, hopeless, but
most humble devotion; there is no dangerous suggestion of
too high an aspiration. Yet the prefatory letter selects
Raleigh as the likeliest to understand the dark conceit of the
magnificent Arthur's love for Gloriana, and this at a time
when Raleigh's near-courtship of the Queen and his
'golden shower' of poems to her were matters of common
knowledge and talk. *Love's Labour's Lost* appeared when
Raleigh was still in disgrace over his marriage with Elizabeth
Throckmorton, and when, in the fourth book of *The
Faerie Queene*, Spenser has done his best to plead for him by
his portrayal of the culprit's grief and anguish. So close a
connection with this epic celebration of magnanimity gives
particular point to the 'magnificence' of Armado, just as the
Cynthia poems are glanced at in his 'mint of phrases', and
Raleigh's worship of the Queen both in Armado's pursuit of
Jaquenetta and his prostration before the Princess to 'adore
her sweet Grace's slipper'. He studies to be a 'complete man'
just as Arthur was a completion of all the virtues. So far as
there was any hint of literary affectation in the cult of
magnanimity, *Love's Labour's Lost* must have delighted its
first audience.

But Armado is a great deal more than a cartoon, however
brilliantly executed. He is a compendium of the fashions,
sartorial and social; he fancies himself too as that familiar
Elizabethan 'character', the melancholy man. He is 'besieged
with sable-coloured melancholy', and inquires of Moth,

'Boy, what sign is it when a man of great spirit grows melancholy?' Perhaps this should warn us not to be too hasty in assessing Shakespeare's attitude, for the melancholy man is one day to reappear as Hamlet; and already there are signs of true magnanimity as well. Like all the great Shakespearian characters, even in motley, Armado is more than an abstract of other men's follies. He is his own delightful self as well, and possibly of all those in the play he endears himself most in the end. The courtiers turn their game to earnest with but little difference of tone; Holofernes returns unlamented to his 'charge house on top of the mountain', and Sir Nathaniel, bless his good heart, to his neighbours and his bowling. But when the schoolmaster, the curate, the clown, and the Don present the pageant of the Nine Worthies to the mocking courtiers (another jest at the heroic tradition) Armado sustains his Hector in the face of fearful odds until unarmed by the news of Jaquenetta's predicament, and finally returns chastened yet magnificent as ever, having 'vowed to hold the plough for her sweet love three year' – the only one of all the lovers unswerving, unmocking, unforsworn.

The whole play is a topical *tour de force*, but even so early, with so tempting a target for his young wit, Shakespeare is in two minds about the cult of magnanimity. The delicious absurdity of the pageant of the Nine Worthies suggests an attack upon the whole text-book theory, as does Doll Tearsheet too when she compares Falstaff to their greatness:

Thou art as valorous as Hector of Troy, worth five of Agemmemnon, and ten times better than the Nine Worthies. (*2 Henry IV*, II iv).

Yet it is the Henry who fooled with Falstaff who becomes his star of England and the flower of chivalry.

Does admiration for the real hero sharpen distaste for any possible sentimentalizing of the magnanimous man? In an intelligently critical mind the balance between admiration and mockery must always be a precarious one, and only the briefest time separates *Henry V* from a satirical attack as savage as *Love's Labour's Lost* was lighthearted – *Troilus and Cressida*. It is not wholly unprepared. Falstaff's catechism of honour – 'Who hath it? He that died o' Wednesday' – has an ugly edge to it, and Doll Tearsheet's Nine Worthies obviously echo a bit of popular fustian. And fustian is just what *Troilus and Cressida* makes of the Greek heroes, whose valour is mostly boasting and railing, a festering corruption of vanity, stupidity, lechery, and treachery. They speak of magnanimity: Helen is

> a theme of honour and renown
> A spur to valiant and magnanimous deeds (II ii 199–200).

and the word rings hollow as a bell in an abandoned church. There are only two men who do not at their every appearance make a mockery of the heroic type, and even they are tarnished. Even Hector's honour is a little specious. He argues on the highest moral grounds for the return of Helen to her husband:

> these moral laws
> Of nature and of nations speak aloud
> To have her back returned. Thus to persist
> In doing wrong extenuates not wrong,
> But makes it much more heavy (II ii 184–8);

yet in the very same breath he casts his vote against her return, rating their 'joint and several dignities' above the law he has just invoked. Troilus himself is described by Ulysses in terms proper to magnanimity:

a true knight;
Not yet mature, yet matchless; firm of word;
Speaking in deeds and deedless in his tongue;
Not soon provoked, nor being provoked soon calmed;
His heart and hand both open and both free;
For what he has he gives, what thinks he shows,
Yet gives he not till judgment guide his bounty,
Nor dignifies an impair thought with breath (IV v 96–103).

But the very next time we see him all this is overthrown by ungovernable fury provoked by a wanton slut. By a final quirk of irony Hector, the man of honour, is treacherously murdered by those who take advantage of his honour; while Troilus, seeking death, finds neither death nor vengeance. The untouched survivors of the play are Pandarus, and Thersites – 'bastard in mind, bastard in valour, in everything illegitimate'.

The sourness of *Troilus and Cressida* is a deadly enough attack upon the heroic type; but it is less insidiously destructive than its opposite development in Jacobean tragedy of the hero whose greatness burns like a fatal star in a black universe. Just as surely as Antony (the magnanimous man *manqué*), these his immediate successors are closely related to epic greatness. But here the dramatist is intent on exploring a wholly different field of human consciousness from that of epic. The epic writer is concerned with the man of noble mind acting or suffering by his own will, in full control of his own actions, moving towards the high purpose to which he is dedicated. But the Jacobean dramatist is fascinated less by man's triumphs than by his failures, less by his greatness than his possible corruption, less by his spiritual freedom than his buffetings by chance, less by his achievements than the fate which he often forges for himself out of his own weaknesses. His purpose may still seem didactic,

material instruction, elegant and sententious excitation t
virtue, and deflection from her contrary, being the soul, limb
and limits of an authentical tragedy,[1]

but the 'material instruction' is warning rather than a spur t
emulation. Chance or fate conspires with human weakness

> We are merely the stars' tennis balls, struck and bandied
> Which way please them.[2]

But it is human weakness which first gives occasion t
chance; like the influence of witchcraft which Byron plead
in self-excuse, it 'can never taint an honest mind'. Play afte
play shows us man at work upon his own destruction
Chapman's Bussy d'Ambois is a man of rare courage an
spirit, but being 'discontent with his neglected worth' h
falls into the fatal error of challenging order itself:

> When I am wrong'd, and that law fails to right me,
> Let me be king myself (as man was made)
> And do a justice that exceeds the law (II ii 197–9).

His Duke of Byron, bulwark of France, is tempted t
treachery through his own vainglory; Webster's Duchess o
Malfi derogates from her own greatness in marrying belov
her worth, and destroys herself as surely as his Vittori
Corombona (the White Devil) burning herself out with he
own baleful lustre. The King who seduces Evadne, i
Fletcher's *The Maid's Tragedy*, prepares his own murder
and Middleton's Beatrice (*The Changeling*) bribing he
servant to kill on her account becomes herself 'the deed'
creature'.

> The abuse of greatness is when it disjoins
> Remorse from power,[3]

[1] Chapman, *The Revenge of Bussy d'Ambois*, Prefatory dedication.
[2] Webster, *The Duchess of Malfi*, V iv 52.   [3] *Julius Caesar*, II i 18–1

and much of the drama of the period is concerned with such a theme, the corruption of the great man by his own power.

It is still greatness which fascinates, but no longer within an ideal world: and, once divorced from the world of ideal virtue, there is a danger that the great man may be confounded with the man of exaggerated courage rather than of true magnanimity. This is certainly so in the tragedies of George Chapman, who probably did more than any other single writer before Dryden to substitute heroics for heroes. His plays are still powerfully impressive, full of trenchant comment upon human life, lit by sudden flashes of poetry which cast a momentary lightning clarity and brilliance over great tracts of the surrounding dark:

> Man is a torch borne in the wind; a dream
> But of a shadow, summ'd with all his substance.[1]

But it is difficult to sympathize fully with Bussy or Byron because it is difficult fully to believe in them. Single-handed they can defeat hosts of enemies; their arrest is dangerous to a whole troop; the single fall of Byron weakens the defence of France itself. Even this we might accept, did not they themselves cherish an idea of their own greatness as exaggerated as that of which Bussy accuses the King's brother:

> all your glories
> Making you terrible, like enchanted flames
> Fed with bare cockscombs (IV, i).

An exception among Chapman's characters is Bussy's brother Clermont in *The Revenge of Bussy d'Ambois*, who is presented as a man of Stoic virtue and composure. He 'speaks all principle'; he can control his passions and

> hath the crown of man in all his parts,
> Which learning is (II, i).

[1] *Bussy d'Ambois.* (I, i).

But he is too often sententious, a Stoic pattern rather than a man who compels our belief, and his personal valour is as exaggerated as in the heroic drama of the Restoration. Few of Chapman's greater characters are completely convincing. There are times when their passions can carry us with them, but it is too short a step from passion to rhetoric. Ear and mind are wearied by the bombast of their self-glorification; and, although Chapman himself condemns it by the despair and fury with which Byron meets his execution, this 'exhalation that would be a star' has so paled all other lights within his orbit that at the end he is still the play's pattern of greatness – and it is a greatness hollow within.

That most formidable and usually generous critic, Dryden, complained of his disappointment on reading *Bussy d'Ambois* after seeing it in the theatre:

> When I had taken up what I had supposed a fallen star, I found I had been cozened with a jelly; nothing but a cold, dull mass, which glittered no longer than it was shooting; a dwarfish thought, dressed up in gigantic words.[1]

It is an astonishing comment from the author of *The Conquest of Granada*. Dryden's heroic drama may have owed much to the theatre of Corneille and Racine; but despite the closing of the English theatres during the Commonwealth there is still an unbroken line of descent, and one cannot underestimate Dryden's debt to the Elizabethan and Jacobean dramatists – and of these he resembles Chapman more than any other! His heroes may not have that 'looseness of expression' of which he accuses his predecessor, but in mood and tone there is very little to choose between the self-glorying of Byron and Almanzor's boast to Almahide:

[1] Preface to *The Spanish Friar*.

Born, as I am, still to command, not sue,
Yet you shall see that I can beg for you;
And if your father will require a crown,
Let him but name the kingdom, 'tis his own.
I am, but while I please, a private man;
I have that soul which empires first began.
From the dull crowd, which every king does lead,
I will pick out whom I will choose to head:
The best and bravest souls I can select,
And on their conquered necks my throne erect[1] (IV, i).

The very care which Dryden takes in his Preface to the play
to justify the extravagance of Almanzor's actions makes one
suspect that he was not quite easy about them. For Almanzor
also, like Byron, is an army in himself. He is warned that

Your slighting Zuelma, this very hour,
Will take ten thousand subjects from your power,

but replies:

What are ten thousand subjects such as they?
If I am scorn'd – I'll take myself away (III, i).

Dryden is in fact attempting the impossible, trying to create
drama in terms of the epic which, as we have seen, proceeds
from a wholly different principle of thought. He makes a
deliberate claim to relate his new heroic drama to heroic
poetry:

An heroic play ought to be an imitation, in little, of an heroic
poem; and, consequently, love and valour ought to be the
subject of it.[2]

But this is a disastrous limitation of the heroic theme. Love
and valour in the true epic sense have a far wider meaning

[1] *The Conquest of Granada.*
[2] *Of Heroique Playes,* 1672 (prefaced to *The Conquest of Granada*).

than that which Dryden gives them in his drama, where love is confined to sexual passion and valour to rash physical courage, expressed in terms of extravagant yet conventional hyperbole. It may be said of his characters, as of Cleopatra, that 'we cannot call their winds and waters sighs and tears; for they are greater storms and tempests than almanacs can report'. But there is little to satisfy one in all this noise. The psychology of passion has been simplified to the point of absurdity. Gone are the inward nobility, and the exquisite complexity of love in all its relationships, to which we are accustomed in the English Renaissance. Dryden's rhetoric has its moments of power, but those who utter it are for the most part posturing shadows; and the predominating tone of false magniloquence is as fatal as satire to true magnanimity.

Thus during the seventeenth century the concept of magnanimity was modified by change within itself at the same time as being weakened from without both by direct satire in comedy and rhodomontade exaggeration in tragedy. But a silent, non-literary, and even more potent cause of decay was the continuous social revolution which is quietly wrought by time itself in any generation. Reverence for heroes is born within an aristocratic society, when the quality of the great leader can be the quality of his country's defences. During the centuries from Alfred to Elizabeth I, one man of courage or vision could carry the fortunes of a whole people in his hands, while a nation was slowly forged by action, warfare, and enterprise. But the 'new men' of Elizabeth's court – the Cecils, the Greshams, and the like – were the portents of a different society, a less youthful and more stable world in which wealth begins to speak as powerfully as action. The later sixteenth century sees the steady growth of a solid middle and merchant class, whose criterion is money. In London, the centre of the literary world, its influence is most obviously apparent, and in one writer after another it is reflected. The clash of the two scales of value, that of romantic heroism and of solid citizenry, makes one of the most farcical comedies of the Elizabethan stage, Beaumont's *Knight of the Burning Pestle*. Ralph, the grocer's apprentice, with his head stuffed full of old tales of chivalry, improvises his own part as an errant knight in a rehearsed play of the portionless apprentice who aspires to his master's daughter; while Ralph's own master and mistress, in the spectator's seats upon the stage, simultaneously applaud his braggadocio speeches and sympathize loudly with the solid citizens and their parental problems and financial anxieties. In this new bustling world of commerce and a growing dependence upon capital, the ideals of a small aristocratic group are likely to be slowly submerged in other interests. Later Elizabethan writers are increasingly fascinated by the spectacle of London itself as it roars past the playhouse door. Ben Jonson takes us straight to the crowded, brawling, cheerful heart of it in *Bartholomew Fair*; he laughs in *The Alchemist* at its rogues, cozeners, and fools; he or Middleton or Chapman will entertain their audiences with the covetousness and ambition of merchant families; Greene anatomizes the confidence trickster and his gull in the *Coney-Catching Pamphlets*. Even serious drama will sometimes concern itself with middle-class characters, as in Heywood's *A Woman killed with Kindness*. The concern of this society is less and less with the Magnanimous Man of an ideal aspiration than with the tragic weakness or comic absurdity of man in his immediate daily surroundings.

For a long while the old and the new will exist side by side. The old, deep-rooted in traditional values, will retain its prestige unless too violently juxtaposed to the new.

Where a writer of sufficient greatness concerns himself with it, it will still command veneration. It is in 1671, eighty years after *The Faerie Queene*, nearly thirty years after the closing of the Jacobean theatres, that the Magnanimous Man appears in his last sunset glory in *Samson Agonistes*. Samson belongs to the epic tradition, the most characteristic form of the age of magnanimity, the world of the heroes. But he appears late, in a period whose most characteristic form is satire, the world of the ordinary man in all his pitiful absurdities. His contemporary is Hudibras, the cowardly braggart knight, with a name borrowed from *The Faerie Queene*, in whom Samuel Butler satirizes Puritan hypocrisy; and only a decade separates him from Dryden's *Absalom and Achitophel*, the mock epic attacking Shaftesbury and the Whig faction, who wished to remove the Duke of York from the succession in favour of the Duke of Monmouth. The central interest of the poem is the wickedly clever presentation of Shaftesbury himself, the man with great potentialities and even noble qualities, but drawn to treason through his own ambitions,

> And all to leave what with his Toil he won
> To that unfeather'd two-legg'd thing, a son.

Ten years divide this from the triumph of Samson, but they are as far apart as the poles of the world. Every period will bring forth its own great men, but the literary age of magnanimity has reached its final close.

SELECT BIBLIOGRAPHY

Some useful editions of the principal authors discussed in the text:

ARISTOTLE: *Ethics*, trans. J. A. K. Thomson (Penguin Classics), 1953.

CHAPMAN: *Works*, 3 vols., ed. R. H. Shepherd, 1874–5, 1889.
Works, ed. W. L. Phelps (Mermaid Series), 1895.
Plays and Poems, 3 vols., ed. T. M. Parrott, 1910–14.

CHAUCER: *Works*, ed. A. W. Pollard *et alia* (Globe ed.), 1898.
Complete Works, ed. F. N. Robinson, Boston, 1933.
Canterbury Tales, trans. N. Coghill (Penguin ed.), 1951.

DRYDEN: *Plays*, 2 vols., ed. G. Saintsbury (Mermaid Series), 1949.

ELYOT: *The Governor*, ed. F. Watson (Everyman's Library), 1907.

GREVILLE, FULKE: *Life of Sir Philip Sidney*, ed. N. Smith, 1907.
The Friend of Sir Philip Sidney (Selections from the *Works*), ed. A. B. Grosart, 1894.

JONSON: *Plays*, 2 vols., ed. B. Nicholson and C. H. Herford (Mermaid Series), 1952.

MALORY: *Works*, 3 vols., ed. E. Vinaver, 1947.
Works, ed. E. Vinaver (Oxford Standard Authors), 1954.
Le Morte D'Arthur, ed. A. W. Pollard (illus. Medici Society ed.), 1927.

MARLOWE: *Works*, ed. C. T. F. Brooke, 1910.

Works, ed. W. L. Phelps, New York, 1912.

Five Plays, ed. Havelock Ellis (Mermaid Series), 1960.

MILTON: *Poetical Works*, ed. H. C. Beeching, 1932.

Poems, 2 vols., ed. H. J. C. Grierson, 1925.

Poetical Works, 2 vols., ed. H. Darbishire, 1952.

Poetical Works, ed. H. Darbishire (Oxford Standard Authors), 1958.

Complete Prose Works, 3 vols., ed. D. M. Wolfe *et alia*, New Haven, 1953–62 (8 vols. projected).

Selected Prose, ed. M. W. Wallace (World's Classics), 1925.

Selected Prose, ed. C. E. Vaughan (Everyman's Library), 1927.

SIDNEY: *Complete Works*, 4 vols., ed. A. Feuillerat, 1923; reprinted 1962.

Apologie, included in *Elizabethan Critical Essays*, 2 vols., ed. G. Gregory Smith, 1904.

SPENSER: *Poems*, ed. J. C. Smith and E. de Selincourt, reprinted 1952.

Works, variorum ed., 11 vols., ed. E. Greenlaw *et alia*, Baltimore, 1932–45.

TRAHERNE: *Centuries, Poems, and Thanksgivings*, 2 vols., ed. H. M. Margoliouth, 1958.

Centuries of Meditations, ed. B. Dobell, reprinted 1950.

INDEX

Note: Titles and characters are entered under the name of the author. Figures in bold face indicate the more important references.

Alexander, 19, 24, **29-31**, 32, 35, 51, 52, 118; *Lives* of, 29, 30, 32

Alfred, King of England, 18, 25, 31, 134

Ariosto, 79; *Orlando Furioso*, 76, 77

Aristotle, **15-17**, 19, 21, 22, 31, 71, 79-80, 82, 84, 85, 92, 93, 104, 107, 112; *Ethics*, 15-17, 20, 80, 81

Arthur, Prince of Wales, 62-3

Ascham, Roger, 72

Aubrey, John, 124

Bacon, Sir Francis, *The Advancement of Learning*, 78; *Of Atheism*, 25-6

Beaumont, Francis, *The Knight of the Burning Pestle*, 135

Beowulf, 28

Bradbrook, M. C., *The School of Night*, 125n.

Butler, Samuel; Hudibras, 136

Castiglione, 72; *The Courtier*, 112

Caxton, William, 51; *The Order of Chivalry*, 49; *Godefrey of Boloyne*, 59; preface to *Morte Darthur*, 76

Cecil family, 117, 124, 134; Hatfield, 117

Chanson de Roland, 28

Chapman, George, 130, 131-3, 135; *Bussy d'Ambois*, 132; *Bussy*, 130, 131; Byron, 130-3 *pass.*; Clermont, 131

Chaucer, Geoffrey, 21, **36-45**, 46, 50, 69, 72, 75, 97, 103; *Dethe of the Duchesse*, 36, 44; *Franklin's Tale*, 39, 41-3, 123; *Knight's Tale*, 38-9, 123; *Man of Law's Tale*, 40n.; *Parson's Tale*, 21; *Second Nun's Tale*, 21, 22; *Squire's Tale*, 40; *Wife of Bath's Tale*, 40, 43

CHARACTERS: Arveragus, 41-2, 51; Aurelius, 41-2; Clerk, 40; Constance, 37, 40n.; Dorigen, 40n., 41-2; Emily, 39; Friar, 40; Franklin, 39, 43, 76; Griselda, 37, 40; Knight, 37, 39, 46; Man in Black, 44, 69; Miller, 37; Palamon and Arcite, 38-9, 51; Squire, 39, 123; Theseus, 38; Sir Topas, 123; Troilus, 37; Wife of Bath, 39

Cicero, *de Officiis*, 17

Dante, 80

Darius, 30, 31
Drake, Sir Francis, 68
Dryden, John, 131, 134; on *Bussy*, 132; *Absalom and Achitophel*, 136; *The Conquest of Granada*, 132-3; Almanzor, 132-3

Elizabeth I, 39, 62, 63, 65, 77, 88, 113, 117, 123-6 *pass.*, 134
Elyot, Sir Thomas, 15, 24, 72; *Bibliotheca Eliotae*, 22; *Governour*, 22, 112
Ethelwerd, 18, 22

Fairfax, Edward, *Godfrey of Bulloigne*, 77
Fletcher, John, *The Maid's Tragedy*, 130
Florence of Worcester, 18

Godeleva, St, 40n.
Greene, Robert, *Coney-Catching Pamphlets*, 135
Gresham, William, 124, 134
Greville, Sir Fulke, 71, 112; *Life of Sidney*, 68, 71, 72
Guy of Warwick, 29

Hall, Joseph, *Characters*, 112
Harington, Sir John, 69; *Briefe Apologie*, 76-7
Havelok the Dane, 29
He bare him up, he bare him down, 48n.
Henry II, 31
Henry VI, 19
Henry, Prince of Wales, 63

Heywood, Thomas, *A Woman Killed with Kindness*, 135
Higford, William, 62n., 112-13; *Institutions*, 112
Hildebert, 17
Hugh de Payens, 47

Institucion of a Gentleman, 25, 112

Joinville, Jean de, 31, 32-5, 112; *Histoire de Saint-Louis*, 32-3
Jonson, Ben, *The Alchemist*, *Bartholomew Fair*, 135; *Masque of Oberon*, 63

King Horn, 29
Knighthood, 35, 46-50
'Knights of Prince Arthur's Round Table', 62

Languet, Hubert, 65
Lee, Sir Henry, 124
Leicester, Earl of, 117
Lewis, C. S., *Allegory of Love*, 86
Louis, St, 32, 33-4, 49, 112
Lydgate, John, *Ballade to Hen. VI*, 19; *Mumming at London*, 19-21, 84; *Troy Book*, 35; *Hector*, 35-6

Magnanimous Man, 16, 20, 80, 93, 104, 107, 112, 113, 116, 118, 122, 135, 136
Magnificence, 19, 20, 22, 63, 79, 83, 91, 96, 125
Malory, Sir Thomas, 37, 45, 46, 49, 72, 75; *Morte Darthur*, 45, **51-61**, 76, 81

CHARACTERS: Arthur, 19, 46, 52, 53-4, 57, 58-60, 62, 63, 69; Blamore, 53; Ector, 57, 60; Galahad, 52, 55, 56, 58; Gareth, 52, 53; Guenevere, 53, 58, 60; Lamorak, 52, 53; Launcelot, 52, 53-4, 56-7, 58, 60, 118; Mark, King of Cornwall, 60, 69; Merlin, 52; Palomides, 52; Tristram and Isoud, 53; Urre, 57; Sangreal, 55, 56

Markham, Francis, *The Book of Honour*, 112

Marlowe, Christopher, *Tamburlaine*, 117-19

Marshal, William, 31, 44n.

megalopsychia, 16, 22, 30, 37, 61, 67, 121

Middleton, Thomas, 135; *The Changeling*, 130

Milles, Thomas, *The Catalogue of Honour*, 62

Milton, John, 26, 31, 67, **94-111**, 112-16 pass., 124; *Areop.*, 99, 108n., *Comus*, 98, 105, 109; *Of Reformation*, 96; *P.L.*, 27, **99-106**, 109, 113; *P.R.*, **107-9**, 113; *S.A.*, **109-11**, 113, 136; *Smectymnuus*, 95, 98; *Tractate of Educ.*, 96

CHARACTERS: Adam, 84, 93, 96, 97, 99-109 pass., 111; Belial, 106; Christ, 55, 93, 107-9; Dalila, 110; Harapha, 110; Mammon, 106; Michael, 96, 102; Samson, 109-11, 136; Satan, 94, 100, 101, 103-6, 107; Zephon, 104

Monumenta Historica Britannica, 18

Nine Worthies, 19, 59, 127, 128

Oakeshott, W., *The Queen and the Poet*, 125n.

L'Ordene de Chevalerie, 47n.

Ormond, Lord, 23

Ovid, *Metamorphoses*, 77

Paul, St, 76, 104

Peele, George, *Polyhymnia*, 62n.

Pelham, Sir William, 74

Perseus, 77

Plato, 38, 80, *Phaedo*, 73

prud'homme, 33-5, 49

Raleigh, Sir Walter, 75, 79, 88, 117, 125-6

Richard I, 29, 30, 31

Roland, 52

Roos, Sir Richard, 19n.

Sainte-Beuve, C.-A., *Causeries de Lundi*, 34

Seaton, M. E., 19n., 50n.

Shaftesbury, Earl of, 136

Shakespeare, 23, 64, **120-9**; *3 Hen. VI*, 23; *J. Caesar*, 121; *L.L.L.*, 24, 124-7; *Meas. for M.*, 64; *M.S.N.D.*, 38; *Tempest*, 64; *Tro. and Cress.*, 24, 128-9

CHARACTERS: Achilles, 24; Antony, 37, 120, 122, 129; Armado, 24, 125-7; Brutus, 121-2; Coriolanus, 120; Doll Tearsheet, 127, 128; Falstaff, 24, 127, 128; Feeble, 24; Fluellen, 24; Hamlet, 127; Hector, 24, 128, 129; Henry V, 122, 127, 128; Jaquenetta,

Shakespeare cont.
    125, 127; Moth, 126; Octa-
    vius, 120; Pandarus, 129;
    Thersites, 129; Troilus, 128,
    129; Ulysses, 128
Shrewsbury, Countess of; Hard-
    wick Hall, 117
Sidney, Sir Philip, 15, 23, 39, **63-74**, 75, 78, 91, 97, 113, 124;
    Apologie, 75, 78; *Arcadia*, **63-73**
  CHARACTERS: Basilius, 64;
    Cleophila, 68; Evarchus, 64,
    66, 69, 70; Gynecia, 64; Musi-
    dorus, 64, 68, 71, 72, 74;
    Pamela, 64, 66, 68, 73;
    Philanax, 69; Philoclea, 64,
    67, 73; Pyrocles, 64, 71-4
    pass.; Tymantus, 69
Sidney, Robert, 15
Skelton, John, *Magnificence*, 84-5
Spenser, Edmund, 22, 26, 37, 38,
    51, 63, 69, 71, 75, 94, 95, 97,
    100, 113, 115, 123-6 *pass.*;
    Faerie Queene, 63, **78-93**, 97,
    115, 126, 136; *Ded. Sonnets*,
    26; prefatory letter, 22, 75,
    79, 125
  CHARACTERS: Acrasia, 85, 86,
    98; Amoret, 86; Amyas, 88;
    Arthegall, 86, 87, 88, 89-90,
    91, 92, 93, 97; Arthur, 79,
    80, 83, 88, 91, 92, 95, 97, 119,
    125, 126; Belphoebe, 88, 125;
    Blandamore, 88; Blatant
    Beast, 38, 90; Braggadochio,
    88; Britomart, 86-7, 88, 90,
    92, 97, 99; Busirane, 86;
    Calidore, 38, 90-1, 97; Cam-
    bell and Triamond, 87; Cori-
    don, 90; Cymochles, 85, 86
    Duessa, 83; false Florimell
    86, 87, 88; Florimell, 86, 87
    Furor, 85; Gloriana, 91, 93
    95, 97, 126; Grantorto, 88;
    Guyon, 67, 85-6, 87, 97, 98;
    Irena, 90; Malbecco, 86, 87;
    Malecasta, 87; Mammon, 85,
    Marinell, 87; Mercilla, 89,
    93; Merlin, 52, 86; Paridell,
    88; Pastorella, 90; Phaedria,
    86; Placidas, 88; Poeana, 88;
    Pyrochles, 85; Red Cross,
    81-4, 97, 118; Scudamore, 86,
    87; Sophy, 91; Talus, 88;
    Thames and Medway, 87;
    Timias, 88, 93, 125; Una, 83,
    84, 93, 97

Tasso, 77, 79
Tournaments, before Edward III,
    62; before Elizabeth, 62n.,
    112-13; 'the Lords and
    Gentlemen that ran', 124
Traherne, Thomas, *Christian
    Ethicks*, 114-15

Upton, Nicholas, 47n.

Villehardouin, Geoffroi de, 31
Vinaver, E., 52, 54

Walsingham, Sir Francis, 67, 70
Waterhouse, Edward, 23
Webster, John; Duchess of Malfi,
    Vittoria Corombona, 130

Yates, F. A., *A Study of Love's
    Labour's Lost*, 125n.